G000255129

TITLE PAGE

EAT | SLEEP | PROPHESY |REPEAT

TOMI ARAYOMI

COPYRIGHT

ISBN 978-0-244-13429-7

DEDICATION AND GRATITUDE

I dedicate this book to my spiritual mum Dr. Sharon Stone who I have had the privilege of knowing since I was eighteen years old. Her compassion, prayers and mentoring are very much the reason I am who I am today. Mum Sharon embodies the prophetic in everything she does and is a modern day general. This book is a memorial to many of the life lessons she has taught and continues to teach me by her example. I love you very much and I am deeply grateful for the years of impartation.

I would like to also appreciate my precious wife, Tahmar India Arayomi, who is not only the amazing mother to our son, Harvey, but is the strongest woman I know on Planet Earth. Thank you for giving me grace and letting me be myself. Thank you for allowing me to go to the Nations and serve the Lord and thank you for serving the Lord with me.

I want to also thank my proofreader and editor Carol Shore-Nye for working tirelessly and with great humility to help me get this book to a publishing standard. I am truly grateful to God for putting you in my path. My life is better for knowing you.

Special thanks goes to Reverend Elliot Cooney who gave me the title for this book.

FOREWORD

If you've ever wondered what your journey into prophetic gifting might look like, this book is for you. Tomi Arayomi brings vitally relevant experiences in an easy to understand & at times humorous way. Because Tomi and I lead a church together, I often get the privilege of receiving from his great revelation and strong prophetic flow. I know you will find inspiration from these pages also.

Dr. Sharon Stone
Founder Christian International Europe

INTRODUCTION

'*Eat Sleep, Prophesy, Repeat,*' is for anyone looking to build their life on the ability to hear God's voice. I grew up in a Catholic home and was very frustrated when we would go to the house of God and hear from everyone but the God of the house. I was fifteen years old when I came to the knowledge of Jesus Christ in a most dramatic and supernatural way. I found out that God doesn't just intend to speak to us but He speaks to us intentionally every day whether we know Him or not. This book is intended to make hearing God's voice a part of every single day of your life by stressing the importance of why Christ came and died. There was a reconciliation plan that Christ had in mind on that Cross, two thousand years ago, that was intended to bring every one of us back into fellowship with God.

Throughout this book, I challenge the Christian reader to accept that God speaks to them every day and I also help provide a map to navigate the auditory signature of God so that they can make experienced guidance from Him a part of their everyday life.

Revelation gives the church a unique advantage over every other institution in the earth today and it is a precious gift from God. Recognising the unique privilege that the church has to access revelation makes us better equipped to engage a dying world in need of a touch from God. God doesn't just want to speak to you, He wants to speak through you.

John 10:27 says, 'My sheep hear My voice!' Simply by starting here, we can end years of conjecture surrounding hearing God's voice. It turns out, God doesn't just want to speak to the Prophets, He wants to speak to you too and daily! He wants you to partner with Him through His Holy Spirit to release Heaven on earth and bring hope to others who don't know that He exists. You can bring edification and encouragement to others around you by learning acknowledging Him daily.

I get the privilege of travelling all over the world telling people what God has to say about them. There is nothing quite like facilitating the critical moment that a soul realises that God knows their intimate secrets. I want to teach others how to hear God and communicate His heart to others. By living everyday conscious of His voice, you too can be a part of facilitating souls coming to the knowledge of Jesus Christ. Learn how to grow in the prophetic ministry, but most importantly, learn how to build the intimacy with the Lord that you have been longing for.

CHAPTER 1 | THE BIRTH OF A PROPHETIC ERA

Revelation gives the church a unique advantage over every other institution in the Earth today and it is a precious gift from God. Recognising the unique privilege that the church has in its access to revelation makes us better equipped to engage a dying world in need of a touch from God. God doesn't just want to speak to you, He wants to speak through you.

John 10:27 says, 'My sheep hear My voice!' Simply by starting here, we can end years of conjecture surrounding hearing God's voice. It turns out, God doesn't just want to speak to the prophets, He wants to speak to you too and daily! He wants you to partner with Him through His Holy Spirit to release Heaven on Earth and bring hope to others who don't know that He exists. You can bring edification and encouragement to others around you by learning to acknowledge Him daily.

From the Book of Acts, Chapter Two (The Day of Pentecost), a new prophetic era has been birthed. However, what if, we as the church, have become so caught up in the experience of Pentecost that we have ultimately, and to our detriment, missed the actual meaning behind it?

In this chapter, we will explore three Defining Moments that led to the birth of this prophetic era. What started off as a desire in the heart of a man called Moses was fulfilled centuries later through a man called Peter. It is a controversial era and one that from its inception sought to end the monopoly on revelation being held in the hands of an elite few forever!

NUMBERS 11:29
29 MOSES SAID TO HIM, "ARE YOU JEALOUS FOR MY SAKE? I WISH THAT ALL THE LORD'S PEOPLE WERE PROPHETS, THAT THE LORD WOULD PUT HIS SPIRIT ON THEM!"

THE END TIME OUTPOURING

JOEL 2:28-29
28 "IT WILL HAPPEN AFTERWARD, THAT I WILL POUR OUT MY SPIRIT ON ALL FLESH; AND YOUR SONS AND YOUR DAUGHTERS WILL PROPHESY. YOUR OLD MEN WILL DREAM DREAMS. YOUR YOUNG MEN WILL SEE VISIONS.
29 AND ALSO ON THE SERVANTS AND ON THE HANDMAIDS IN THOSE DAYS, I WILL POUR OUT MY SPIRIT.

The Bible speaks of a time that God will do something He has never done before. It was the church in the Book of Acts that became the prophetic marker for this unprecedented move. This time has since become known as Pentecost. However, what really transpired on that fateful day in that upper room was more than just the birthing of what would later be known as the precursor to the Pentecostal movement. It just so happened, that what the Lord did that day prophetically coincided with a Jewish celebration called Pentecost, but the events of that day were, as they are now, obscure and miscommunicated! For indeed of that day it was said by some:

ACTS 2:12-13
12 THEY WERE ALL AMAZED, AND WERE PERPLEXED, SAYING ONE TO ANOTHER, "WHAT DOES THIS MEAN?"
13 OTHERS, MOCKING, SAID, "THEY ARE FILLED WITH NEW WINE."

11 HE SAID, "GO OUT, AND STAND ON THE MOUNTAIN BEFORE THE LORD." BEHOLD, THE LORD PASSED BY, AND A GREAT AND STRONG WIND TORE THE MOUNTAINS, AND BROKE IN PIECES THE ROCKS BEFORE THE LORD; BUT THE LORD WAS NOT IN THE WIND. AFTER THE WIND AN EARTHQUAKE; BUT THE LORD WAS NOT IN THE EARTHQUAKE.
12 AFTER THE EARTHQUAKE A FIRE PASSED; BUT THE LORD WAS NOT IN THE FIRE: AND AFTER THE FIRE A STILL SMALL VOICE.

It is easy in the midst of a move of God to get so caught up in the hysteria that the intentions of the Holy Spirit become miscommunicated or somehow conflated with the effects of His Presence. What if we are defining "Pentecost" by the effects of His coming and not by His intention for coming? What if, the church today have gotten so caught up in the experience of the earthquake, the fire and the wind of God that we have sensationalised the moment, worshipped the experience and ultimately missed the true meaning of it? I don't believe that, 'forgetting the reason for the season' can merely be relegated to Christmas. For indeed, some of the same elements of earth, wind and fire that Elijah experienced in 'the Lord passing by' reflect some of the same elements and experiences that the New Testament believers encountered in that upper room.

ACTS 2:1-3
1 NOW WHEN THE DAY OF PENTECOST HAD COME, THEY WERE ALL WITH ONE ACCORD IN ONE PLACE.
2 SUDDENLY THERE CAME FROM THE SKY A SOUND LIKE THE RUSHING OF A MIGHTY WIND, AND IT FILLED ALL THE HOUSE WHERE THEY WERE SITTING.

3 TONGUES LIKE FIRE APPEARED AND WERE DISTRIBUTED TO THEM, AND ONE SAT ON EACH OF THEM.

BUT THE LORD WAS NOT IN...

The day of Pentecost is by and large accepted by the church as being when the believers in the Upper Room were filled with the Spirit with the evidence of tongues. The world then, just as today, defined them as a bunch of crazy drunks, chanting and making noise. What really took place on that day has been lost in the drama of the manifestations. That day was indeed earth shaking, wind howling and fire filled but that should not be confused with Pentecost's Defining Moment! In essence, what if, just like in the case of Elijah, the Lord was not in the fire, the wind or the earthquake?

Peter was quick to bring clarity to both the pioneering church, which was a baby on that day, and the ever spectating and skeptical world. This clarity helps both the spectator and the partaker navigate exactly where they are on God's calendar. I call this spiritual landmark a *'Defining Moment.'*

Peter stopped the debate on Pentecost by saying that this is what a prophet had foretold. That there would come a time where the Spirit of God would end denominationalism, schisms, sectarianism and religious control, and thereby ending centuries of revelation being monopolised by the few. The prophet Joel had prophesied that the Spirit of God would do something unprecedented – He would breach dogmatic structures and humanistic religious protocols to instead

engage every single person on the face of planet earth!
Children, young men, old men, women, servants, employees –
all will hear the voice of God and no one will be with excuse on
that day of judgment!

All flesh did not mean, all Christian flesh. Acts 2 was not about
the believer, it was about the unbeliever!

ACTS 2:14-18
**14 BUT PETER, STANDING UP WITH THE ELEVEN, LIFTED UP
HIS VOICE, AND SAID UNTO THEM, YE MEN OF JUDEA, AND
ALL YE THAT DWELL AT JERUSALEM, BE THIS KNOWN UNTO
YOU, AND HEARKEN TO MY WORDS:
15 FOR THESE AREN'T DRUNKEN, AS YOU SUPPOSE, SEEING
IT IS ONLY THE THIRD HOUR OF THE DAY.
16 BUT THIS IS WHAT HAS BEEN SPOKEN THROUGH THE
PROPHET JOEL:
17 'IT WILL BE IN THE LAST DAYS, SAYS GOD, THAT I WILL
POUR OUT MY SPIRIT ON ALL FLESH. YOUR SONS AND YOUR
DAUGHTERS WILL PROPHESY. YOUR YOUNG MEN WILL SEE
VISIONS. YOUR OLD MEN WILL DREAM DREAMS.
18 YES, AND ON MY SERVANTS AND ON MY HANDMAIDENS IN
THOSE DAYS, I WILL POUR OUT MY SPIRIT, AND THEY WILL
PROPHESY.**

THE FIRST DEFINING MOMENT | HOLY SPIRIT SALVATION

John 20 was the first recorded defining moment for the church.
For it was here that the first significant Holy Spirit Defining
Moment was about to take place. Being born again!

22 AND WHEN HE HAD SAID THIS, HE BREATHED ON THEM, AND SAITH UNTO THEM, RECEIVE YE THE HOLY GHOST:

John 20:22 was the first Defining Moment. It was here that Jesus wrought salvation through the indwelling Holy Spirit. Whilst John 20:22 marked salvation through accepting Jesus Christ's message, Acts 2 dealt more with a release of power that would birth salvation. Salvation was the result of Acts 2; the instant result of power Christianity was that souls would be saved. In John 20:22 they received the Presence of Jesus in their hearts; in Acts 2 they received the Power of Jesus upon their bodies.

Pentecost was not about keeping God in an upper room, nor even was Pentecost about speaking in tongues. Pentecost, according to Peter, was to fulfil an ancient prophecy that God would never give a human being on planet earth a reason to say, "God did not speak to me!"

Is it possible that we today have become so preoccupied with the effects of Pentecost that we have monumentalised the moment and missed the meaning?

10 I FELL DOWN BEFORE HIS FEET TO WORSHIP HIM. HE SAID TO ME, "LOOK! DON'T DO IT! I AM A FELLOW BONDSERVANT WITH YOU AND WITH YOUR BROTHERS WHO HOLD THE TESTIMONY OF JESUS. WORSHIP GOD, FOR THE TESTIMONY OF JESUS IS THE SPIRIT OF PROPHECY."

Here we see Apostle John seeing an angel and worshipping the experience! The angel, being of God, was quick to rebuke him. I believe that encountering God can sometimes be so

14

glorious that we can quite easily fall into John's error of worshipping the moment, the angel, the fire, that we miss the meaning. The Bible says, 'the testimony of Jesus' or the '*marturia*' meaning the '*evidence*' of Jesus is the Spirit of Prophecy.

Every Christian brother and sister should be united in our joint ability to hear the voice of God. Christ's intention in sending the Holy Spirit was so that every single person on the face of the Earth could have this testimony or evidence. The evidence or proof that Jesus is in a room is not the manifestation of tongues, but the manifestation of prophecy! When people start prophesying, know that Jesus is in the room!

1 CORINTHIANS 14:23-25
23 IF THEREFORE THE WHOLE ASSEMBLY IS ASSEMBLED TOGETHER AND ALL SPEAK WITH OTHER LANGUAGES, AND UNLEARNED OR UNBELIEVING PEOPLE COME IN, WON'T THEY SAY THAT YOU ARE CRAZY?
24 BUT IF ALL PROPHESY, AND SOMEONE UNBELIEVING OR UNLEARNED COMES IN, HE IS REPROVED BY ALL, AND HE IS JUDGED BY ALL.
25 AND THUS THE SECRETS OF HIS HEART ARE REVEALED. SO HE WILL FALL DOWN ON HIS FACE AND WORSHIP GOD, DECLARING THAT GOD IS AMONG YOU INDEED.

THE SECOND DEFINING MOMENT | BEING PROPHETIC AGAIN WITH THE EVIDENCE OF TONGUES!

Some today believe that speaking in tongues is the evidence of being born again. The Apostles were not born again in Acts, they were born again in the Book of John. Speaking in tongues is the evidence that prophecy, revelation (dreams & visions), interpretation and words of knowledge live in you and are waiting to get out of you! Greater is the one that prophesies than the one that speaks in tongues.

1 CORINTHIANS 14:5-6
5 I WOULD THAT YE ALL SPAKE WITH TONGUES, BUT RATHER THAT YE PROPHESIED: FOR GREATER IS HE THAT PROPHESIETH THAN HE THAT SPEAKETH WITH TONGUES, EXCEPT HE INTERPRET, THAT THE CHURCH MAY RECEIVE EDIFYING.
6 NOW, BRETHREN, IF I COME UNTO YOU SPEAKING WITH TONGUES, WHAT SHALL I PROFIT YOU, EXCEPT I SHALL SPEAK TO YOU EITHER BY REVELATION, OR BY KNOWLEDGE, OR BY PROPHESYING, OR BY DOCTRINE?

Tongues are encoded prophecies, revelations, words of knowledge and doctrines waiting for you to decode the mystery and release them as a sound of distinction!

1 CORINTHIANS 14:1-5
1 FOLLOW AFTER LOVE, AND EARNESTLY DESIRE SPIRITUAL GIFTS, BUT ESPECIALLY THAT YOU MAY PROPHESY.
2 FOR HE WHO SPEAKS IN ANOTHER LANGUAGE SPEAKS NOT TO MEN, BUT TO GOD; FOR NO ONE UNDERSTANDS; BUT IN THE SPIRIT HE SPEAKS MYSTERIES.

3 BUT HE WHO PROPHESIES SPEAKS TO MEN FOR THEIR EDIFICATION, EXHORTATION, AND CONSOLATION.
4 HE WHO SPEAKS IN ANOTHER LANGUAGE EDIFIES HIMSELF, BUT HE WHO PROPHESIES EDIFIES THE ASSEMBLY.
5 NOW I DESIRE TO HAVE YOU ALL SPEAK WITH OTHER LANGUAGES, BUT RATHER THAT YOU WOULD PROPHESY. FOR HE IS GREATER WHO PROPHESIES THAN HE WHO SPEAKS WITH OTHER LANGUAGES, UNLESS HE INTERPRETS, THAT THE ASSEMBLY MAY BE BUILT UP.

The reason the assembly is not being built up is nothing to do with our evangelism programs nor our night vigils or prayer movements! The reason the assembly is not growing is because prophecy is no longer the fundamental part of our services. We gather to speak in tongues, to preach, to take offerings but the singular purpose of coming to the house of God ought to be to hear from the God of the house a now and Rhema (living) Word that transcends sermonising. The Church, as an institution becomes redundant when it omits the prophetic. Revelation is the very foundation and capstone on which the New Testament Church is composed.

MATTHEW 16:17-18
17 JESUS ANSWERED HIM, "BLESSED ARE YOU, SIMON BAR JONAH, FOR FLESH AND BLOOD HAS NOT REVEALED THIS TO YOU, BUT MY FATHER WHO IS IN HEAVEN.
18 I ALSO TELL YOU THAT YOU ARE PETER, AND ON THIS ROCK I WILL BUILD MY ASSEMBLY, AND THE GATES OF HADES WILL NOT PREVAIL AGAINST IT.

THE THIRD DEFINING MOMENT | THE ALL FLESH MOVEMENT

When Joel said that all flesh would prophesy, He meant that The Holy Spirit was going to create an environment where it would be near impossible for people to say, 'I never knew!' or 'I never heard!' This is what Apostle Paul meant in the Book of Hebrews when He said:

HEBREWS 8:10-11
10 FOR THIS IS THE COVENANT THAT I WILL MAKE WITH THE HOUSE OF ISRAEL AFTER THOSE DAYS, SAITH THE LORD; I WILL PUT MY LAWS INTO THEIR MIND, AND WRITE THEM IN THEIR HEARTS: AND I WILL BE TO THEM A GOD, AND THEY SHALL BE TO ME A PEOPLE:
11 AND THEY SHALL NOT TEACH EVERY MAN HIS NEIGHBOUR, AND EVERY MAN HIS BROTHER, SAYING, KNOW THE LORD: FOR ALL SHALL KNOW ME, FROM THE LEAST TO THE GREATEST.

Paul is not trying to make the preaching and teaching ministry obsolete. Far from it, we still need preachers, teachers and evangelists. Salvation through Jesus Christ is still the only way to the Father. What he is saying in this Scripture is that this New Covenant unlike the Old One where revelation was limited to a few, is now being spread abroad from the least to the greatest. We need Apostles, Prophets, Evangelists, Pastors and Teachers to facilitate the experience, not to create the experience!

The Bible speaks in Acts 10 of a man called Cornelius. He was a Roman centurion in the Italian regiment. He was not born again and he was not Jewish, yet he was doing all the things a

Christian should do.

ACTS 10:2
2 A DEVOUT MAN, AND ONE WHO FEARED GOD WITH ALL HIS HOUSE, WHO GAVE GIFTS FOR THE NEEDY GENEROUSLY TO THE PEOPLE, AND ALWAYS PRAYED TO GOD.

Cornelius was God fearing. He did not know which God to fear but he seemed to fear a God he did not yet even know. He gave generously and prayed to God regularly! Could this phenomenon be what Paul was speaking about that God would begin to write His law on human hearts?

ROMANS 2:14-15
14 (FOR WHEN GENTILES WHO DON'T HAVE THE LAW DO BY NATURE THE THINGS OF THE LAW, THESE, NOT HAVING THE LAW, ARE A LAW TO THEMSELVES,
15 IN THAT THEY SHOW THE WORK OF THE LAW WRITTEN IN THEIR HEARTS, THEIR CONSCIENCE TESTIFYING WITH THEM, AND THEIR THOUGHTS AMONG THEMSELVES ACCUSING OR ELSE EXCUSING THEM)

Cornelius becomes the first fruit and the second 'Defining Moment' of what Joel meant by *'ALL FLESH!'*

ACTS 10:3
3 AT ABOUT THE NINTH HOUR OF THE DAY, HE CLEARLY SAW IN A VISION AN ANGEL OF GOD COMING TO HIM, AND SAYING TO HIM, "CORNELIUS!"

In the vision of the angel, Cornelius is told to send for a man called Peter who lives in a beach house at Joppa. When the whole thing was explained to Peter and he finally went to Cornelius, he was amazed and said:

19

ACTS 10:34-35
34 **"TRULY I PERCEIVE THAT GOD DOESN'T SHOW FAVOURITISM;**
35 **BUT IN EVERY NATION HE WHO FEARS HIM AND WORKS RIGHTEOUSNESS IS ACCEPTABLE TO HIM.**

Peter, who was the first spokesman for the second Defining Moment after being born again (that the Spirit of God would be poured out on all flesh) did not understand the ramification of *'all flesh'* meaning all flesh, saved and unsaved, Jewish and Gentile, circumcised and uncircumcised. Up until this time there had been no expectation or thought that a gentile could be saved, let alone be received by the Holy Spirit. Peter's theology and indeed the early churches theology was irreversibly elasticated.

ACTS 10:44-48
44 **WHILE PETER WAS STILL SPEAKING THESE WORDS, THE HOLY SPIRIT FELL ON ALL THOSE WHO HEARD THE WORD.**
45 **THEY OF THE CIRCUMCISION WHO BELIEVED WERE AMAZED, AS MANY AS CAME WITH PETER, BECAUSE THE GIFT OF THE HOLY SPIRIT WAS ALSO POURED OUT ON THE GENTILES.**
46 **FOR THEY HEARD THEM SPEAKING IN OTHER LANGUAGES AND MAGNIFYING GOD. THEN PETER ANSWERED,**
47 **"CAN ANY MAN FORBID THE WATER, THAT THESE WHO HAVE RECEIVED THE HOLY SPIRIT AS WELL AS WE SHOULD NOT BE BAPTIZED?"**
48 **HE COMMANDED THEM TO BE BAPTIZED IN THE NAME OF JESUS CHRIST. THEN THEY ASKED HIM TO STAY SOME DAYS.**

Peter realised something! He had a third Defining Moment. First- be born again, second- The Spirit of revelation through dreams, visions and prophecy ending the monopoly on revelation and third- all flesh means all flesh- Salvation by being baptised in the Name of Jesus is the product of the goodness of God being demonstrated through revelation.

The third Defining Moment in Apostle Peter's life was a vision
he had on the roof of his beach house in Joppa.

ACTS 10:10-17
10 HE BECAME HUNGRY AND DESIRED TO EAT, BUT WHILE
THEY WERE PREPARING, HE FELL INTO A TRANCE.
11 HE SAW HEAVEN OPENED AND A CERTAIN CONTAINER
DESCENDING TO HIM, LIKE A GREAT SHEET LET DOWN BY
FOUR CORNERS ON THE EARTH,
12 IN WHICH WERE ALL KINDS OF FOUR-FOOTED ANIMALS
OF THE EARTH, WILD ANIMALS, REPTILES, AND BIRDS OF
THE SKY.
13 A VOICE CAME TO HIM, "RISE, PETER, KILL AND EAT!"
14 BUT PETER SAID, "NOT SO, LORD; FOR I HAVE NEVER
EATEN ANYTHING THAT IS COMMON OR UNCLEAN."
15 A VOICE CAME TO HIM AGAIN THE SECOND TIME, "WHAT
GOD HAS CLEANSED, YOU MUST NOT CALL UNCLEAN."
16 THIS WAS DONE THREE TIMES, AND IMMEDIATELY THE
VESSEL WAS RECEIVED UP INTO HEAVEN.
17 NOW WHILE PETER WAS VERY PERPLEXED IN HIMSELF
WHAT THE VISION WHICH HE HAD SEEN MIGHT MEAN,
BEHOLD, THE MEN WHO WERE SENT BY CORNELIUS, HAVING
MADE INQUIRY FOR SIMON'S HOUSE, STOOD BEFORE THE
GATE,

The Outpouring came first

It is very interesting to me how the man who gave the
revelation in Acts 2 could not even conceive the day God
would pour out His Spirit on the Gentile (non-Jewish)
community. Notice that salvation in this case did not come until
after the outpouring! Cornelius' house had already
encountered the goodness of God through this outpouring

(dreams and visions) but they needed wisdom and revelation to help them come into an understanding of what they were experiencing.

An unsuspecting sinner collided with an unsuspecting saint and the two unbeknownst to each other were instruments in a far bigger move than either of them could have ever conceived. A move that meant the Lord would speak first and ask questions later!

The goodness of God that leads to repentance

In the church today, we are guilty of trying to clean people up and get them saved. We have this salvation mentality. Don't get me wrong, evangelism is vital. Every Christian believer must do the work of an evangelist (2 Timothy 2:5) even if they are not necessarily an evangelist.

However, in the New Testament, it is not repentance that leads to the goodness of God, rather it is the goodness of God that leads to repentance! When we switch from a salvation mentality to a goodness of God mentality, salvation will be the natural by-product of demonstrating the goodness of God.

ROMANS 2:4
4 OR DO YOU DESPISE THE RICHES OF HIS GOODNESS, FORBEARANCE, AND PATIENCE, NOT KNOWING THAT THE GOODNESS OF GOD LEADS YOU TO REPENTANCE?

We are still living under John the Baptist's ministry when we lead by repentance and not by the goodness of God. My uncle

Bishop Fred Addo put it to me like this, "You cannot skin the fish you haven't caught yet."

I've heard many preachers mock prophetic evangelism and I have sat in the meetings of great revivalists who have condemned prophecy for the unbeliever as 'fortune-telling' and foolish. Having been in the prophetic ministry for over 16 years, I can tell you that the prophetic is not for the church solely, but for the unbeliever. When the church gets prophetic again we will see people fall on their knees and exclaim, "God is among you!"

1 CORINTHIANS 14:24-25
24 BUT IF ALL PROPHESY, AND SOMEONE UNBELIEVING OR UNLEARNED COMES IN, HE IS REPROVED BY ALL, AND HE IS JUDGED BY ALL.
25 AND THUS THE SECRETS OF HIS HEART ARE REVEALED. SO HE WILL FALL DOWN ON HIS FACE AND WORSHIP GOD, DECLARING THAT GOD IS AMONG YOU INDEED.

MUHAMMAD MY UBER

I was in Amsterdam with my twin brother at a European Gathering of Prophets. That night we prophesied with a group of prophets over around 200 people. We left the conference hall at around 11pm at night exhausted. My brother called an Uber driver named Muhammad to come pick us up. It didn't take a rocket scientist to figure out of what faith he was. Muhammad was amazed that we had been in church for so long and asked us what we were doing there till that late in the night. My brother proceeded to tell Muhammad about the love of Jesus, the Gospel and the Cross.

I could tell Muhammad appreciated my brother's intentions, but that to him Allah was far greater and he only appreciated Jesus as a prophet. I looked over to my brother and tapped him and whispered, quite frustratedly, "Prophecy to the man!" My brother sharply responded, "You do it!" As you can imagine this lasted for a good while until Mohammed asked the question, "So what do you both do?"

I saw this as my opening and quickly responded, "Muhammad, we get the awesome privilege of telling people what Jesus is saying about them. Would you like to hear what He says about you?"

Muhammad laughed and excitedly said "Yes please", not knowing what he had just invited. From the back seat my brother and I touched his shoulder and we prophesied.

"Muhammad, the Lord knows you have tried to make money righteously and even left school early to be your own man, but you have found some unrighteous ways to make money that have got you in trouble with the authorities and God wants to show you mercy."

We were interrupted by the satnav which was saying to turn left. Muhammad ignored the satnav and opted for taking the long way back to our hotel.

He screamed, "Yes brothers, I am in trouble with the judge because I got caught selling drugs, Pray to God for me to show me mercy."

We talked all the way home and prayed for him. We said, "Now Muhammad, God is going to do it for you because He is good – but if you want to know Him, when you get home, pray and just ask Him to show Himself to you."

We don't know if Muhammad ever did give his life to Christ, but I am one hundred percent convinced that God turned his case around. Why? Because God is good. Not because we believe in Him, but because He is good!

ROMANS 3:3-4
3 FOR WHAT IF SOME WERE WITHOUT FAITH? WILL THEIR LACK OF FAITH NULLIFY THE FAITHFULNESS OF GOD? 4 MAY IT NEVER BE! YES, LET GOD BE FOUND TRUE, BUT EVERY MAN A LIAR. AS IT IS WRITTEN, "THAT YOU MIGHT BE JUSTIFIED IN YOUR WORDS, AND MIGHT PREVAIL WHEN YOU COME INTO JUDGMENT."

ALL FLESH - THE RAMIFICATIONS OF A NEW OUTPOURING

This outpouring of the Holy Spirit is falling upon the Matthews in the church and the Muhammads in the mosque. God, by His Holy Spirit, will invade the night and day space of individuals all over the world from the least to the greatest to give no one an excuse not to know Him.

We see evidence of the Holy Spirit throughout the Old Testament releasing prophecy over the lives of people who you nor I would consider worthy.

In Genesis, the Pharaoh was a self-aggrandising, narcissist.

He worshipped himself as a reincarnate god. The serpent was the prominent symbol of Egypt and still is to this day. Yet the Lord saw fit to pour out His Spirit upon Pharaoh and give him a dream. Joseph was not there to create or convict; his job was like Peter to bring clarity to what the Spirit of God was saying and doing.

GENESIS 41:25
25 AND JOSEPH SAID UNTO PHARAOH, THE DREAM OF PHARAOH IS ONE: GOD HATH SHEWED PHARAOH WHAT HE IS ABOUT TO DO.

If this is what happened when the Spirit of God was limited in operation, imagine what will happen in this new day, end time outpouring of the Holy Spirit. Let us now come into a full understanding that the Holy Spirit is going to come upon the church and upon the world. He does not have sides nor show partiality!

CHAPTER 2 | BEFORE I FORMED YOU I KNEW YOU

THE IDENTICAL DREAM OF THE IDENTICAL TWINS

The Lord called me to His ministry when I was just a fifteen-year-old boy. My personal first Defining Moment happened one fateful night when my identical twin brother and I, with an identical brain, got an identical exam result. We had both failed an exam that would determine the quality of school we would attend in the United Kingdom, a country that my parents fought tooth and nail to get into. This exam would not only determine our intellectual future, but for my parents, it embodied the long offset hope that their efforts to emigrate from Nigeria to the UK was not in vein.

Our failure not only reflected poorly on us, but it embarrassed our parents for whom success then was paramount and failure was a stain on the successful family name. The failure we felt that day converted into a suicide pact that we individually, and unbeknownst to the other, had made, not with each other as twins, but with God. In the backyard of our family home we prayed an identical prayer that would affect the rest of our lives forever.

In our desperation we individually yet identically cried to the heavens, "God, if you're real, show yourself to me tonight or I will kill myself!"

That same night we individually yet identically prepared ourselves mentally for the next day where we would end our lives and pondered quietly on how to painlessly fulfil our mission. A meditation neither of us discussed with each other. I had managed to cry myself to sleep and that's when the dream started.

In my dream, I crawled through a tiny hole in my house. It was a miracle that I got through considering my body mass at the time was quite large. I came out the other side relieved, but I was no longer in my home. I was standing at the back of a crowd of people all chanting loudly. The crowd was so large that it was literally a sea of people.

I was immediately transported onto the stage where I (the fifteen-year-old me) saw myself. The version of myself was a little bit older, taller and skinnier. I was talking loudly to the crowd with gusto and bravado. Large shafts of brilliant light would pour out upon the people as I spoke and the atmosphere was filled with joy.

I began to listen in on the chants of the people and the more I listened the more coherent their outcry became. "Jesus! Jesus! Jesus!", they chanted.

Angrily, I said within myself (the fifteen-year-old me), "Can they not see it is not Jesus on that stage, but Tomi!" Out of the corner of my eye came a brilliant being of pure white light with a figure I could not make out. I just knew it was the Lord, yet I have no idea how I knew that. His presence was pure light, a light that penetrates skin, bones and goes right through to the soul of a man.

Out of the brilliance of the light a beautiful voice spoke, "My Son, you asked Me and this is what I have called you to!"

I woke up from the dream, my brother woke up! I sat up, my brother sat up! At the same time, we said,

"I had a dream, you had a dream, you go first, okay... I'll go first... hahahaha!"
"I had a dream, you had a dream, you go first, okay... I'll go first... hahahaha!"

My brother explained that he crawled through a tiny hole in our house only to see a large crowd. He was transported onto a stage where he saw himself only older. The older version of himself was speaking with great boldness and shafts of light were falling on the people. He then proceeded to explain how angry he was at them chanting "Jesus, Jesus..." Whilst he explained, my eyes and mouth were wide open. He proceeded to talk about the being of white light that said, "My son, you asked Me and this is what I have called you to!"

From that fateful day, we decided to serve the Lord and from one prophetically identical dream, we decided to give our whole lives to Jesus Christ. It was not an altar call, not a theology school, but a revelation in a dream from Jesus to two young boys that changed our lives forever.

CREATION VERSUS FORMATION

For a long time, I felt like young Jeremiah in the Bible who some scholars say was a seventeen year old boy when God called him to the prophetic ministry. He began his ministry at a time when the incumbent king, Josiah, was only 22 years old. Being called at fifteen, I understood the immense pressure that Jeremiah was under at the time of His calling. For one, he had parents who like mine had ambitions for him. He was at an age of sexual curiosity and trying figuring out his social orientation in a heavily congested sociological orbit that all gravitationally preferred evil. He had peers who were dating and falling in love and living the typical teenage life. He was forming zits in unfortunate places, on his nose, and blackheads on his forehead. He had no idea who he wanted to be and was likely trying to find a job so he could move out of his parents' basement and become his own man. In the midst of all that, God shows up and says:

JEREMIAH 1:5-7
5 "BEFORE I FORMED YOU IN THE BELLY, I KNEW YOU. BEFORE YOU CAME FORTH OUT OF THE WOMB, I SANCTIFIED YOU. I HAVE APPOINTED YOU A PROPHET TO THE NATIONS."

Jeremiah responds:

6…"AH, LORD THE LORD! BEHOLD, I DON'T KNOW HOW TO SPEAK; FOR I AM A CHILD."

Then the Lord says,

7 ..."DON'T SAY, 'I AM A CHILD;' FOR TO WHOEVER I SHALL SEND YOU, YOU SHALL GO, AND WHATEVER I SHALL COMMAND YOU, YOU SHALL SPEAK.

How is it possible for God to know me before He formed me? How is it possible that before I was even born, God appointed me as a prophet! Jeremiah wasn't the only one to encounter this phenomena. David said,

PSALM 139:16
16 YOUR EYES SAW MY UNFORMED SUBSTANCE; IN YOUR BOOK WERE WRITTEN, EVERY ONE OF THEM, THE DAYS THAT WERE FORMED FOR ME, WHEN AS YET THERE WAS NONE OF THEM.

How did God know an unformed me? Does that mean that there are two versions of Tomi and one is a substance in a test tube somewhere being held by God and ordained to something he had no intention of becoming?

THE BOOK OF GENE-SIS

The Book of Genesis is a book of the Gene pool of God. It is the story of our DNA, where we came from and how we became who we are. It offers great understanding of Jeremiah 1 where God says, "Before I formed you I knew you." For indeed it is both the story of creation and the story of formation to whoever will understand it.

Genesis is God creating earth as a parallel world of heaven! In other words, the earth is a parallel dimension that was made to mirror perfectly and reflect heaven. This is why when Jesus teaches us how to pray He says:

MATTHEW 6:10
10 LET YOUR KINGDOM COME. LET YOUR WILL BE DONE, AS IN HEAVEN, SO ON EARTH.

Earth is a parallel dimension, made to mirror heaven perfectly! So in Genesis 1, God creates plant kind.

GENESIS 1:11
11 GOD SAID, "LET THE EARTH YIELD GRASS, HERBS YIELDING SEED, AND FRUIT TREES BEARING FRUIT AFTER THEIR KIND, WITH ITS SEED IN IT, ON THE EARTH"; AND IT WAS SO.

God literally gets the genome for plant-kind from heaven and mirrors it on earth.

GENESIS 1:12
12 THE EARTH YIELDED GRASS, HERBS YIELDING SEED AFTER THEIR KIND, AND TREES BEARING FRUIT, WITH ITS SEED IN IT, AFTER THEIR KIND; AND GOD SAW THAT IT WAS GOOD.

When God says, "It was good", he was doing quality assurance testing to ensure that the plant-kind in heaven mirrored the plant-kind on earth.

God creates:
* Plant-kind (Genesis 1:12)
* Marine-kind, insect-kind and bird-kind (Genesis 1:21)
* Animal-kind (Genesis 1:24)

Everything God made was good! Meaning that it mirrored

Heaven perfectly! God had made everything on Earth as it was in Heaven, yet one thing was missing. A vital gene pool so royal it could rule worthily over this perfect and harmonious, parallel ecosystem.

LET US MAKE US

GENESIS 1:26-27
26 GOD SAID, "LET US MAKE MAN IN OUR IMAGE, AFTER OUR LIKENESS: AND LET THEM HAVE DOMINION OVER THE FISH OF THE SEA, AND OVER THE BIRDS OF THE SKY, AND OVER THE LIVESTOCK, AND OVER ALL THE EARTH, AND OVER EVERY CREEPING THING THAT CREEPS ON THE EARTH." 27 GOD CREATED MAN IN HIS OWN IMAGE. IN GOD'S IMAGE HE CREATED HIM; MALE AND FEMALE HE CREATED THEM.

In this parallel dimension, God creates a mirror image of Himself! Since God is Spirit, the being of Genesis 1:26 was a spirit. In fact, the very word "image" is the Hebrew word *Tselem* meaning a phantom or a ghost.

JOHN 4:24
24 GOD IS SPIRIT, AND THOSE WHO WORSHIP HIM MUST WORSHIP IN SPIRIT AND TRUTH."

Genesis 1:26 marks a significant moment in history. The Lord God created a parallel version of Himself and gave this parallel being a king-dominion over the Earth just as His counterpart (otherwise known as '*the Last an Adam*' 1 Corinthians 15:45) ruled heaven! This Adam ruled in a parallel that I will call 'the 4th dimension.'

Adam lived in a dimension outside of the formed world. We call it the 4th dimension (even though it was Adam's first dimension) because we have no concept of it. He existed outside of the space-time continuum. In this continuum, also lived God, angels and one known as The Word, Who would Himself later take on a three dimensionality of His own! He was there in the Beginning.

JOHN 1:1
1 IN THE BEGINNING WAS THE WORD, AND THE WORD WAS WITH GOD, AND THE WORD WAS GOD.

JOHN 1:14
14 THE WORD BECAME FLESH, AND LIVED AMONG US. WE SAW HIS GLORY, SUCH GLORY AS OF THE ONE AND ONLY SON OF THE FATHER, FULL OF GRACE AND TRUTH.

FROM 4D ADAM to 3D ADAM

Adam was a man of dual citizenship. He was the only one of God's creation that travelled between two parallel universes. In Genesis 2:7, the Lord puts His new earth king into a body, citing that:

GENESIS 2:7
7 THE LORD GOD FORMED MAN FROM THE DUST OF THE GROUND, AND BREATHED INTO HIS NOSTRILS THE BREATH OF LIFE; AND MAN BECAME A LIVING SOUL.

The Lord God took a man from outside of the space-time continuum in Genesis 1:26 and put him into the space-time continuum in Genesis 2:7. In Genesis 2, we see the incarnate

Genesis 1 man just like in the Book of John we see the incarnate Word who would later be known as Jesus.

ADAM (4th Dimension)	ADAM (3rd Dimension
Spirit	Flesh and Soul
Creation	Formation
Born of God	Formed of Dust
Blessed	Cursed
Dominion	Domestic
Mission	Sub-Mission
Life	Death
Lived	Existed
Assignment	Employment
Talks to God	Talks to humans and others but can't hear God
Prophetic	Pathetic

CREATION VS FORMATION

Adam was created in Genesis 1 and formed in Genesis 2. He lived in the fourth dimension (God dimension) meaning that he was superior (a god of the 3rd and lesser parallel universe). Adam did not see in the spirit, he saw from the spirit. Creation revered him because he lived in a dimension that was greater than theirs. He was the only creation of God capable of trans-+existence. Imagine a being totally consumed in a dimension outside of the 3D world that we know, to the point that he himself had no knowledge that he had a three dimensional body.

GENESIS 2:25
25 THEY WERE BOTH NAKED, THE MAN AND HIS WIFE, AND WERE NOT ASHAMED.

The fourth dimension is a place of multi-dimensionality, far beyond our understanding. Adam did not see this dimension in pictures, visions or dreams. His spirit body was able to appreciate multi-dimensional space without need for interpretation, revelation or mysticism. As long as he lived outside of the dimension of his rulership, he would maintain his dominion over creation forever.

One fateful day, the enemy seized opportunity through Adam's wife to set in motion a scandalous affair that would eternally doom Adam's descendants to a prison formally known to us today as the flesh (third dimension or formation.)

GENESIS 3:6-7
6 WHEN THE WOMAN SAW THAT THE TREE WAS GOOD FOR FOOD, AND THAT IT WAS A DELIGHT TO THE EYES, AND THAT THE TREE WAS TO BE DESIRED TO MAKE ONE WISE, SHE TOOK OF ITS FRUIT, AND ATE; AND SHE GAVE SOME TO HER HUSBAND WITH HER, AND HE ATE.
7 THE EYES OF BOTH OF THEM WERE OPENED, AND THEY KNEW THAT THEY WERE NAKED. THEY SEWED FIG LEAVES TOGETHER, AND MADE THEMSELVES APRONS.

This treasonous act by the serpent (Satan) robbed Adam and Eve of the place where they were created and literally land locked them to the place where they were formed. Earth days became birthdays as man for the first time opened his formed eyes and was 'born again', only this time in to a lesser parallel

36

dimension. The lion no longer feared him and simply saw him as all lions see humans – as flesh!

Now we understand why The all-knowing Lord comes walking in the garden in the cool of the day and proclaims:

GENESIS 3:8-9
8 THEY HEARD THE VOICE OF THE LORD GOD WALKING IN THE GARDEN IN THE COOL OF THE DAY, AND THE MAN AND HIS WIFE HID THEMSELVES FROM THE PRESENCE OF THE LORD GOD AMONG THE TREES OF THE GARDEN.
9 THE LORD GOD CALLED TO THE MAN, AND SAID TO HIM, "WHERE ARE YOU?"

How is it that the Omniscient God could not find His creation? Because His creation had lost the part of them that lived in His dimension. Much is to be said for the word 'cool of the day'. If we are not careful we would assume that the Bible was simply giving us weather report. The word cool is the Hebrew word *'ruach'* it means - spirit!

So let's read it again:

GENESIS 3:8-9
8 THEY HEARD THE VOICE OF THE LORD GOD WALKING IN THE GARDEN IN THE SPIRIT OF THE DAY, AND THE MAN AND HIS WIFE HID THEMSELVES FROM THE PRESENCE OF THE LORD GOD AMONG THE TREES OF THE GARDEN.
9 THE LORD GOD CALLED TO THE MAN, AND SAID TO HIM, "WHERE ARE YOU?"

The reason the Lord could not find Adam was because He was not looking for Adam in the 3D world, He was looking for Adam in his creation and yet found a fallen Adam in his formation.

37

Not fallen by latitude, but fallen by dimensionality.

Adam became a prisoner of the world over which he was called to rule! His brain, heart and body were sensatory, but certainly not spiritual. For God, talking to a 3D Adam was as futile as a man talking to a dog. You had to train it and teach it a few words, but you could never fully communicate with it like you once did.

Adam was no longer living in his creation, but in his formation. No more did Adam see life from the Spirit. If Adam was ever to see life, he would have to see in the spirit from the flesh ruled by a lesser intellectual mind.

God would have to explain four dimensional concepts to a three dimensional generation, using tangible things within their dimension as teachable things to explain concepts outside of their dimension.

JOHN 3:10-12
**10 JESUS ANSWERED HIM, "ARE YOU THE TEACHER OF ISRAEL, AND DON'T UNDERSTAND THESE THINGS?
11 MOST CERTAINLY I TELL YOU, WE SPEAK THAT WHICH WE KNOW, AND TESTIFY OF THAT WHICH WE HAVE SEEN, AND YOU DON'T RECEIVE OUR WITNESS.
12 IF I TOLD YOU EARTHLY THINGS AND YOU DON'T BELIEVE, HOW WILL YOU BELIEVE IF I TELL YOU HEAVENLY THINGS?**

It would eventually mark a day where for God to even explain Himself to mankind would mean that He would have to leave his higher dimension and deliberately come into our lesser dimension. This is the reason for the Cross!

HEBREWS 2:14
**14 SINCE THE CHILDREN HAVE FLESH AND BLOOD, HE TOO
SHARED IN THEIR HUMANITY SO THAT BY HIS DEATH HE
MIGHT BREAK THE POWER OF HIM WHO HOLDS THE POWER
OF DEATH-- THAT IS, THE DEVIL--**

The mission of Christ was simple. To bring us back to life again
and redeem the life to us that the enemy had stolen from us!

JOHN 10:10
**14 THE THIEF COMES ONLY TO STEAL AND KILL AND
DESTROY; I HAVE COME THAT THEY MAY HAVE LIFE, AND
HAVE IT TO THE FULL.**

When Adam sinned he was born again, but only this time as a
fallen man. When Christ came, His message was to be born
again, but this time back into the Spirit from which we had
fallen.

JOHN 3:5-7
**5 JESUS ANSWERED, "MOST CERTAINLY I TELL YOU, UNLESS
ONE IS BORN OF WATER AND SPIRIT, HE CAN'T ENTER INTO
THE KINGDOM OF GOD!
6 THAT WHICH IS BORN OF THE FLESH IS FLESH. THAT WHICH
IS BORN OF THE SPIRIT IS SPIRIT.
7 DON'T MARVEL THAT I SAID TO YOU, 'YOU MUST BE BORN
AGAIN.'**

JEREMIAH'S CALL IS ALL OUR CALL

JEREMIAH 1:4-5
4 NOW THE WORD OF THE LORD CAME TO ME, SAYING,
5 "BEFORE I FORMED YOU IN THE BELLY, I KNEW YOU.
BEFORE YOU CAME FORTH OUT OF THE WOMB, I SANCTIFIED
YOU. I HAVE APPOINTED YOU A PROPHET TO THE NATIONS."

This is where I conclude this chapter!

It was important for us to understand our Genesis or rather our "Gene-sis" before I explained the title of this chapter. Now you will have a clearer understanding of this verse of scripture. This is not God having a conversation with Jeremiah-the-formation (Genesis 2:7), God is trying to have a conversation with Jeremiah-the-creation (Genesis 1:26).

He says to Jeremiah (paraphrased), "You may not know this but there is a version of you I created to hear My voice and prophecy to nations. Jeremiah, you were created to hear Me!"

Reader! You were created to hear God long before you were formed! Adam and Eve were not Apostles, Prophets, Evangelists, Pastors or Teachers. They were so much more, they were spirits created to hear and have fellowship with God. They were a prophetic people, who had access to the very heart, mind and conscience of the Lord God Himself.

In Jeremiah 1, God was having a duo dialogue. He was in full conversation with Jeremiah-the-creation, but Jeremiah-the-formation kept speaking up! That man of the flesh, limited and primitive, who's intellect is to God utter foolishness, spoke up and had the audacity to say:

JEREMIAH 1:6
6 THEN I SAID, "AH, LORD THE LORD! BEHOLD, I DON'T KNOW HOW TO SPEAK; FOR I AM A CHILD."

DON'T LET MY FORM CON YOU!

What's your excuse for not speaking up? Are you too young, too old, too black, too white, too sick, too poor, too rich, too much, too depressed, too grieved, too empty, too full, too popular, too unknown, too mean, too friendly, too overbearing, too underwhelming, too married, too single, too stupid, too smart, too fat, too short, too skinny, too tall, too pregnant, too barren, too busy, too lazy?

Whatever your excuse, I want you to remember this, "Don't let your form con you!"
Memorialise that, write it down somewhere so that every time you or others give you an excuse or try to limit you to what they see and what you see in the mirror, you can remember that the mirror will never truly be a reflection of the real you! You were made in a much bigger image than what the mirror reflects. You were created in an image beyond the mirror; so much deeper than superficial characteristics.

Paul in Romans says this,

ROMANS 12:2

2 DON'T BE **CONFORMED** TO THIS WORLD, BUT BE TRANSFORMED BY THE RENEWING OF YOUR MIND, SO THAT YOU MAY PROVE WHAT IS THE GOOD, WELL-PLEASING, AND PERFECT WILL OF GOD.

In other words, Paul was trying to say, "Do not let your form con you!"
You are so much bigger than anything that can exist in this world. You were created by God to be literally 'out of this world!" When God conceived you, He did not imagine you as a form but as a created being in His image and after His likeness.
A spirit, that like Jeremiah, can hear His voice and know His call for your life. Do not let your form con you and rob you of your true dimension! Before God formed you, He knew a version of you that He created for dominion. You and I will never have that dominion again as long as we let our form con us into living a life absent of the voice of God!

Are you ready to stop being conned by your form to sin, to fornicate, to lie, to commit adultery, to watch pornography and do all the things that make you feel worthless? The truth is, the flesh is worthless but the spirit is worthwhile!

Those who are looking for worth in the flesh will never find it! You were not made to live in the flesh and its biggest con is to convince those who are trying to live life to the full that the flesh is capable of making them full. Indeed, the flesh will quench your taste, but as with all fizzy drinks it will never quench your thirst!

JOHN 6:63
63 IT IS THE SPIRIT WHO GIVES LIFE. THE FLESH PROFITS
NOTHING. THE WORDS THAT I SPEAK TO YOU ARE SPIRIT,
AND ARE LIFE.

Nations are waiting, destiny is calling but not for the formed
man but for the created man. Are you ready, oh man and
woman of the flesh, to become a man and woman of the
Spirit?

JOHN 3:3-6
3 JESUS ANSWERED HIM, "MOST CERTAINLY, I TELL YOU,
UNLESS ONE IS BORN AGAIN, HE CAN'T SEE THE KINGDOM
OF GOD."
4 NICODEMUS SAID TO HIM, "HOW CAN A MAN BE BORN
WHEN HE IS OLD? CAN HE ENTER A SECOND TIME INTO HIS
MOTHER'S WOMB, AND BE BORN?"
5 JESUS ANSWERED, "MOST CERTAINLY I TELL YOU, UNLESS
ONE IS BORN OF WATER AND SPIRIT, HE CAN'T ENTER INTO
THE KINGDOM OF GOD!
6 THAT WHICH IS BORN OF THE FLESH IS FLESH. THAT WHICH
IS BORN OF THE SPIRIT IS SPIRIT.

If so, repeat after me,

> *Father,*
>
> *I come to you asking you for forgiveness for all my*
> *sins. I now understand why you came to take me out of*
> *the form that's conned me into living life beneath the*
> *life that you created me for. I know now that I can only*
> *come back to you through your Son Jesus Christ, who*
> *so loved me that He took on form and died for me so*

that death would not be the end and the dust that formed me would not one day claim me as its prisoner. I receive the price your Son paid and I accept it. Take me back into the Spirit so I can be born again, born spirit again, born to hear and see again, born to talk to you again, born to serve you again. Not from my flesh but from My Spirit!

In Jesus Name, Amen.

CHAPTER 3 | THE ANATOMY OF THE PROPHETIC

MY FIRST PROPHET ENCOUNTER

When I was around eighteen years old, my brother and I co-planted over twelve churches in the United Kingdom and were pastoring its base in Hertfordshire University whilst studying law. Many of our students were getting ready to leave the university church as most UK courses are three years long. I did not want them to go into the world without having some kind of encounter or moment with the Lord where they could hear for themselves His plans for them post university life. One day, I was in my university dorm room when I asked the Lord this question.

His response to me was simple, "Tomi, it's time to call for the prophets."

I had always known myself to be prophetic yet, it seemed to me that God spoke to me in short intervals (now known to me as words of knowledge). Students, saved and unsaved heard the folklore about twin pastors who could tell them what they did last night. Whether all the legends were true or not remains to be tested, but most certainly, many of these stories were exaggerated.

Hearing the voice of God, although in soundbite format was quite easy for me. I remember I could honestly (and foolishly) go for days without prayer and still be able to hear the voice of God. I never quite understood it, but I could have a day or an entire month of compromise (being young there was plenty of opportunity for) and yet God would still speak with Me as if we were picking up where we left off and nothing was ever wrong.

When people would tell me that they struggled to hear God, it was a foreign concept to me. I didn't just hear God, I encountered Him often in visions during my youth. When He told me to send for the prophets, I prayed to Him for understanding for months as 'prophet' was not quite my terminology at the time to define what it was I was doing.

One defining day, I was invited by a friend of mine to a conference with my twin brother and our ministry team. A woman called Denise Baize from New York was speaking that night about the prophetic. I will never forget her as long as I live! She was speaking with such boldness about the prophetic and was the first woman I ever encountered who shamelessly called herself a prophet and not presumptively! Her abilities matched her acclaim as she stood my brother and I up and for the next twenty minutes proceeded to "read our mail." She prophesied effortlessly and whereas my ability to prophesy was in soundbites, hers were in whole sentences. Each one began with, "The Lord says…" Don't get me wrong, I am not referring to a style, I am referring to an authority.

My prophecies were never prefixed by 'The Lord says…' It was far too risky to associate my words with the word of the Lord! I preferred to say, "I saw you last night in a vision…" Her fearless authority was awe inspiring and gave me a hunger not just for what she said, but the authority with which she said it!

She said it as if she was God's mouthpiece.

MEETING SHARON STONE

The next day, I had heard that a woman called Sharon Stone was preaching. I thought to myself, I didn't know the actress was a Christian! I went to the meeting expecting to find another bold strong prophet only to find this short white lady. When I say short, I mean less than five feet tall. I remember them giving her a block to stand on just so she could be visible on the platform. It was easy for me to be conned by her form. Out of her tiny body came a roaring voice of a lioness with the gentleness of a lamb. She was a complete paradox, short in form yet tall in spirit! She spoke with authority and a clarity of her calling as a prophetess that I had never seen nor heard before nor since.

It turned out that Dr. Sharon Stone (as she was fondly known) was just as famous in Christian circles as her actress namesake. Again, just like the night before, my brother and I were first to be called up for prophecy. She spoke things into our lives that, to date, are still shaping the course of our destinies irreversibly.

She prophesied for what felt like thirty minutes and each word was loaded with content and the very love of God. She spoke into the mistakes of our youth, but not with exposure although I knew she had the ability. Rather, she wrapped each word carefully in the love of God to give us just enough exposure to the Father's heart without exposing us to the crowd around us.

encountered anyone like Dr. Sharon Stone!
_ .ʋɪd me, "Son, behold your mother!" I would come to know years later that the Lord told her that I was her spiritual son and that she was to raise me up as a man of God.

To date, I have the privilege of co-pastoring a church in Windsor UK with my spiritual mum, Dr. Sharon Stone. I invited her to the university church all those years ago and once again she reproduced not only the accurate prophetic words, but also the love of God that wrapped each word without diminishing the content. She was not in it for Mum Sharon, she was in it for Jesus! I would observe times the Lord would speak to her about pornography or adultery in people's lives, that she would stop publicly prophesying and ask to see the person after the meeting. She would sit them down and in the love of God restore them quickly. I would observe grateful faces who knew that she had the capacity to pull the reputation trigger and wreck lives from the pulpit but she carried the prophetic with an essence of apology. Not apology for who she was, but apology for what the prophetic had done to harm and wound God's people. A love and compassion that now coats my prophetic ministry and is one of her many impartations into my life.

THE FOUR PROPHETIC ANATOMIES

In no chronology I want to talk about the four anatomies of the prophetic. I want to explain why some find it easier to hear God than others and that we are all called to at least one or more than one faculty.

1. The Spirit of prophecy
2. The gift of prophecy
3. The office of The Prophet
4. The friend of God

---

1. THE SPIRIT OF PROPHECY

REVELATION 19:10
10 I FELL DOWN BEFORE HIS FEET TO WORSHIP HIM. HE SAID TO ME, "LOOK! DON'T DO IT! I AM A FELLOW BONDSERVANT WITH YOU AND WITH YOUR BROTHERS WHO HOLD THE TESTIMONY OF JESUS. WORSHIP GOD, FOR THE TESTIMONY OF JESUS IS THE SPIRIT OF PROPHECY."

John, like many of us, fell prey to worshipping the moment. He bowed down to an angel and got so caught up in the moment that the angel had to remind him of the meaning for the encounter.

He said the testimony, evidence or witness of Jesus in a room is the Spirit of prophecy. In essence, "Be born again with the evidence of prophecy" The Holy Spirit is a prophet! It is His first office to prophesy and point to Jesus. Every new born believer is born into the realm of the person of the Holy Spirit. Just like Adam we are born in the Spirit and the Spirit is a person and He is a realm. Just like a fish needs water to swim, we need the realm of the Holy Spirit to hear the voice of God!

The Holy Spirit governs the fourth dimension in the earth, He aligns our bodies in the Spirit so that our born again spirits can fellowship with God.

2 CORINTHIANS 13:14
14 **THE GRACE OF THE LORD JESUS CHRIST, THE LOVE OF GOD, AND THE FELLOWSHIP OF THE HOLY SPIRIT, BE WITH YOU ALL. AMEN.**

Adam lived in the realm of the person of the Holy Spirit and that is how He was able to communicate with the Lord. When we are born of the Spirit of God, we have access back to the Father through the Spirit who knows the mind of the Father. The Spirit of Prophecy lives in the born again believer as 'revelation', but He also operates not in the world but on the world in a format known as prophecy. The two are not the same thing! Revelation belongs only to the children of God, prophecy belongs to the saved and unsaved!

A dream is a prophecy, a vision is a prophecy, but a revelation is the demystifying of dreams and visions - a realm that God has always kept the world from!

DEUTERONOMY 29:29
29 **THE SECRET THINGS BELONG TO THE LORD OUR GOD; BUT THE THINGS THAT ARE REVEALED BELONG TO US AND TO OUR CHILDREN FOREVER, THAT WE MAY DO ALL THE WORDS OF THIS LAW.**

When God gives a dream to a king or an unsaved loved one for instance, God is not revealing Himself, God is concealing Himself! It is for His children (the born again spirit) to reveal secrets which are foolishness to the world!

1 CORINTHIANS 2:14

14 NOW THE NATURAL MAN DOESN'T RECEIVE THE THINGS OF GOD'S SPIRIT, FOR THEY ARE FOOLISHNESS TO HIM, AND HE CAN'T KNOW THEM, BECAUSE THEY ARE SPIRITUALLY DISCERNED.

When the Bible says that the natural man does not receive the things of God's Spirit, it does not mean that God does not engage with the unsaved and natural man, He means that the natural man has no comprehension of what He is truly receiving and the fact that it is from God. It takes a spiritual man to explain spiritual things to natural (unspiritual) people.

GENESIS 41:25

25 JOSEPH SAID TO PHARAOH, "THE DREAM OF PHARAOH IS ONE. WHAT GOD IS ABOUT TO DO HE HAS DECLARED TO PHARAOH.

In Genesis 41:25, God shows Pharaoh Egypt's future by the Holy Spirit. This was not by the indwelling presence of the Holy Spirit of the New Testament by reason of which we are born again. This was by the Spirit of Prophecy whom Joel foretold would come upon all flesh, both spiritual and unspiritual. This is not a realm where man comes to the knowledge of God but where God comes into the knowledge of man!

The Spirit of Prophecy is, according to Revelation 19:10, the evidence of Jesus Christ in the room. The Prophet Joel calls it, "The outpouring".

JOEL 2:28-29

28 "IT WILL HAPPEN AFTERWARD, THAT I WILL POUR OUT MY SPIRIT ON ALL FLESH; AND YOUR SONS AND YOUR DAUGHTERS WILL PROPHESY. YOUR OLD MEN WILL DREAM DREAMS. YOUR YOUNG MEN WILL SEE VISIONS.

29 AND ALSO ON THE SERVANTS AND ON THE HANDMAIDS IN THOSE DAYS, I WILL POUR OUT MY SPIRIT.

The outpouring will be a season where the Holy Spirit will invade the chambers of children, old men, youth, kings, presidents, Imams, Sikhs, witches, house helps, butlers, waiters, door keepers, Republicans, Democrats, Tories and Labour. The indwelling Holy Spirit has a bias, but when the same Holy Spirit that is within the born-again believer is poured out upon the world, we call this, "The Spirit of Prophecy" and this realm has no bias.

JOHN 16:8
8 WHEN HE HAS COME, HE WILL CONVICT THE WORLD ABOUT SIN, ABOUT RIGHTEOUSNESS, AND ABOUT JUDGMENT;

The Spirit of Prophecy is contagious, He manifests most in the midst of worship. You will begin to notice that as you lift up the name of Jesus, the Spirit of Prophecy tends to manifest through regular congregants who, all of a sudden, feel a bursting need to share something.

JEREMIAH 20:9
9 IF I SAY, I WILL NOT MAKE MENTION OF HIM, NOR SPEAK ANY MORE IN HIS NAME, THEN THERE IS IN MY HEART AS IT WERE A BURNING FIRE SHUT UP IN MY BONES, AND I AM WEARY WITH FORBEARING, AND I CAN'T.

This urge to share is the contagious atmosphere created when worshipping Jesus. A lot of churches do not yet know what to do with this atmosphere other than the typical weighing of what the member has to share and then giving them freedom to share it.

Often the member who is sharing it can quite easily disrupt the flow of the service and not because God is not speaking to them, but because they have not yet learned to turn revelation into prophecy (because the two are different things) they end up sharing the revelation and feel redundant when their words feel inconsequential.

The awkward pastor-to-congregant relationship surrounding the Spirit of Prophecy will continue to go on for as long as there is no thorough understanding of how to engage with the Spirit of Prophecy when He fills an atmosphere. It is possible that with well-meaning intentions, we can grieve and even quench the Holy Spirit by despising the prophecies of our congregations.

It is just as equally possible that a congregant may have a word that simply does not come from the Lord. So often what happens to us as pastors, is we would rather for the sake of protecting our flock, quench the fire (unknowingly) by stopping all prophecy or controlling it, rather than create a free-for-all open mike night where unfettered and unaccountable words can potentially cause harm. We, as pastors must learn to weigh prophecy and become facilitators of it. This is something we will discuss later on. Paul admonishes us not to quench the Holy Spirit by despising prophecy.

1 THESSALONIANS 5:19-21
19 **DON'T QUENCH THE SPIRIT.**
20 **DON'T DESPISE PROPHESIES.**
21 **TEST ALL THINGS, AND HOLD FIRMLY THAT WHICH IS GOOD.**

CONTAGIOUS

In the Bible, we hear of a young man called Saul who was about to become a king. Samuel, who ordained Saul told him that he was getting ready to come into a company of prophets. Let's read what happened when he did:

1 SAMUEL 10:5
5 "AFTER THAT YOU SHALL COME TO THE HILL OF GOD, WHERE IS THE GARRISON OF THE PHILISTINES: AND IT SHALL HAPPEN, WHEN YOU HAVE COME THERE TO THE CITY, THAT YOU SHALL MEET A BAND OF PROPHETS COMING DOWN FROM THE HIGH PLACE WITH A PSALTERY, AND A TAMBOURINE, AND A PIPE, AND A HARP, BEFORE THEM; AND THEY WILL BE PROPHESYING:

1 SAMUEL 10:10-11
10 WHEN THEY CAME THERE TO THE HILL, BEHOLD, A BAND OF PROPHETS MET HIM; AND THE SPIRIT OF GOD CAME MIGHTILY ON HIM, AND HE PROPHESIED AMONG THEM. 11 IT HAPPENED, WHEN ALL WHO KNEW HIM BEFORE SAW THAT, BEHOLD, HE PROPHESIED WITH THE PROPHETS, THEN THE PEOPLE SAID ONE TO ANOTHER, "WHAT IS THIS THAT HAS COME TO THE SON OF KISH? IS SAUL ALSO AMONG THE PROPHETS?"

Saul was not a prophet. However, when he came into prophetic company and they were worshipping God, the Spirit of Prophecy would on Saul and he would begin to prophesy. Why? Because the Spirit of prophecy is contagious. You and I can participate in an outpouring for our own neighbourhoods just by releasing an atmosphere of worship in our houses. The outpouring of the Holy Spirit is a generational promise! If you can steward an atmosphere within your neighbourhood through praise and worship, you will be shocked when your neighbours start talking to you about strange dreams they had (likely with you in it).

You can become a beacon of the Spirit of Prophecy within your home by changing the atmosphere, taking discreet prayer walks around your neighbourhood and creating an atmosphere for an outpouring.

ACTS 1:8
8 BUT YOU WILL RECEIVE POWER WHEN THE HOLY SPIRIT HAS COME UPON YOU. YOU WILL BE WITNESSES TO ME IN JERUSALEM, IN ALL JUDEA AND SAMARIA, AND TO THE UTTERMOST PARTS OF THE EARTH."

By participating with the Holy Spirit, who is not limited to a church building, we can release an atmosphere over our Jerusalem, Judea and Samaria that will cause people living in the world (people like Cornelius in the book of Acts) to have dreams and visions.

2. THE GIFT OF PROPHECY

The gift of prophecy is given by the Holy Spirit to the born-again believer. The Holy Spirit does not give gifts to people who are not born-again. Think of the gift of prophecy like a birthday gift when you give your life to Jesus Christ.

Not every believer has a gift of prophecy, but Paul said every believer should covet above all nine gifts of the Spirit (written about in 1 Corinthians 12) the gift of prophecy!

1 FOLLOW AFTER LOVE, AND EARNESTLY DESIRE SPIRITUAL GIFTS, BUT ESPECIALLY THAT YOU MAY PROPHESY.

THE DIFFERENCE BETWEEN THE SPIRIT OF PROPHECY AND THE GIFT OF PROPHECY

The Spirit of Prophecy is for the world and the church. When the Holy Spirit is poured out it is a sovereign move of His Spirit that no human being alive can control. Not even Apostle Peter himself could facilitate the outpouring of the Spirit of Prophecy upon the Gentile house of Cornelius and was amazed that God forewent Peter's theology and order to reach a man who was the least likely man and family to be touched.

The gift of prophecy (like all the nine gifts of the Spirit) however is given by the Spirit of God to the born again believer for the building up of the local church!

1 CORINTHIANS 12:4-12
4 NOW THERE ARE VARIOUS KINDS OF GIFTS, BUT THE SAME SPIRIT.
5 THERE ARE VARIOUS KINDS OF SERVICE, AND THE SAME LORD.
6 THERE ARE VARIOUS KINDS OF WORKINGS, BUT THE SAME GOD, WHO WORKS ALL THINGS IN ALL.
7 BUT TO EACH ONE IS GIVEN THE MANIFESTATION OF THE SPIRIT FOR THE PROFIT OF ALL.
8 FOR TO ONE IS GIVEN THROUGH THE SPIRIT THE WORD OF WISDOM, AND TO ANOTHER THE WORD OF KNOWLEDGE, ACCORDING TO THE SAME SPIRIT;
9 TO ANOTHER FAITH, BY THE SAME SPIRIT; AND TO ANOTHER GIFTS OF HEALINGS, BY THE SAME SPIRIT;
10 AND TO ANOTHER WORKINGS OF MIRACLES; AND TO ANOTHER PROPHECY; AND TO ANOTHER DISCERNING OF

SPIRITS; TO ANOTHER DIFFERENT KINDS OF LANGUAGES; AND TO ANOTHER THE INTERPRETATION OF LANGUAGES. 11 BUT THE ONE AND THE SAME SPIRIT WORKS ALL OF THESE, DISTRIBUTING TO EACH ONE SEPARATELY AS HE DESIRES. 12 FOR AS THE BODY IS ONE, AND HAS MANY MEMBERS, AND ALL THE MEMBERS OF THE BODY, BEING MANY, ARE ONE BODY; SO ALSO IS CHRIST.

When the Spirit of God gives gifts, these gifts do not work *upon* the believer, these gifts work *within* the New Testament believer. Unlike the Spirit of Prophecy which stirs you up, you must stir up the gift of prophecy.

2 TIMOTHY 1:6
6 FOR THIS CAUSE, I REMIND YOU THAT YOU SHOULD STIR UP THE GIFT OF GOD WHICH IS IN YOU THROUGH THE LAYING ON OF MY HANDS.

You cannot control the Holy Spirit, but you can control the gift!

1 CORINTHIANS 14:32
32 THE SPIRITS OF THE PROPHETS ARE SUBJECT TO THE PROPHETS,

The Spirit of Prophecy can be taken away by grief, vexation and sorrow (Isaiah 63:10), but the gift of prophecy will never be taken away even if the person backslides.

ROMANS 11:29
29 FOR THE GIFTS AND THE CALLING OF GOD ARE IRREVOCABLE.

I can neglect the gift, but I cannot kill the gift. In essence I can become a bad steward of the gift God has given me and not work it out through Godly training. It never becomes a dead spiritual muscle, just a weak one. Many Christians can energise their gift in a moment where they need it most because, like all muscles, the gift of prophecy has muscle memory, so it can be re-engaged during crisis. It is important that you and I learn to constantly work out our gift and not to neglect it.

1 TIMOTHY 4:14
14 DON'T NEGLECT THE GIFT THAT IS IN YOU, WHICH WAS GIVEN TO YOU BY PROPHECY, WITH THE LAYING ON OF THE HANDS OF THE ELDERS.

The Spirit of Prophecy is God manifesting upon you. The gift of prophecy is God manifesting within you. This is why, when you are operating under the Spirit of Prophecy, you will feel emotions, but will not necessarily feel tired afterwards, whereas when you are operating from the gift within you, then you are doing the work as God's Spirit enables you. The gift is physically and psychologically demanding; it is a gift of grace, but you labour under it.

1 CORINTHIANS 15:10
10 BUT BY THE GRACE OF GOD I AM WHAT I AM. HIS GRACE WHICH WAS BESTOWED ON ME WAS NOT FUTILE, BUT I WORKED MORE THAN ALL OF THEM; YET NOT I, BUT THE GRACE OF GOD WHICH WAS WITH ME.

The gifts are part of your equipment, but the Spirit is part of your DNA! The more time you spend with the Spirit of Prophecy the more you energise the gift of prophecy.

20 BUT YOU, BELOVED, KEEP BUILDING UP YOURSELVES ON YOUR MOST HOLY FAITH, PRAYING IN THE HOLY SPIRIT.

GIFT OF PROPHECY	SPIRIT OF PROPHECY
Saved	Saved and unsaved
Within	Upon
Stirred up	Stirs me up
Imparted	Invaded
Within my control	Without my control
Can be neglected	Can be grieved
I work by Him	He works by me
Irrevocable	Revocable
For the church to build the church	For the saved and unsaved to build the world as God intended
Given by grace	Given because of grace
Cannot be quenched	Can be quenched
Subjected	Sovereign

The above chart demonstrates some of the key differences.

3. THE OFFICE OF THE PROPHET

There is a lot to be said for those in the office of a prophet and even more to be said of the online conjecture on digital spaces surrounding this area of ministry. Many believe that this office does not exist and is a mere relic relegated to the Old

Testament of the Bible. For quite some time in the Body of Christ, the office of the Prophet has been confused with the gift of prophecy; which is to edify the church. After all, we can't have people going around saying, "The Lord says", it's far too dangerous and has the capacity to create control, not to mention the unforetold havoc the prophetic office has already waged throughout the centuries.

For fear of false prophets, church leaders have made the monumental move of excusing all prophets as a safety net for their flock. However, by doing so, they have removed the very foundation stone upon which the Satan-proof church is supposed to be built.

EPHESIANS 2:20
20 BEING BUILT ON THE FOUNDATION OF THE APOSTLES AND PROPHETS, CHRIST JESUS HIMSELF BEING THE CHIEF CORNERSTONE;

The foundation stone of the church is the apostolic and prophetic ministry. It is this stone that has by and large been treated as an add-on that must be restored back to the sub-level infrastructure of the church if it is to be an unbeatable end time force. Institutions will be shaken (education, media, government, family, entertainment, business) but there is a promise for the church institution built on the right rock and it is this:

MATTHEW 16:18
18 I ALSO TELL YOU THAT YOU ARE PETER, AND ON THIS ROCK I WILL BUILD MY ASSEMBLY, AND THE GATES OF HADES WILL NOT PREVAIL AGAINST IT.

Author and respected Bible teacher Dr. Tim Hamon speaks expressively about this statement that Christ made to Peter. It has led to the formation of many man-made edifices and grand architectures like St Paul's Cathedral in London. Dr. Tim explains that the reason Christ was in a building mood was purely because of a question Jesus asked and an answer Peter (then Simon) gave.

MATTHEW 16:13
13…"WHO DO MEN SAY THAT I, THE SON OF MAN, AM?"

Everybody offers their ideas, but Peter says something truly transcendent that seems to get Jesus' attention.

MATTHEW 16:16
16 SIMON PETER ANSWERED, "YOU ARE THE CHRIST, THE SON OF THE LIVING GOD."

Anybody reading this would not expect it to provoke the kind of response it provoked in Jesus, Who said.

MATTHEW 16:17-19
17 JESUS ANSWERED HIM, "BLESSED ARE YOU, SIMON BAR JONAH, FOR FLESH AND BLOOD HAS NOT REVEALED THIS TO YOU, BUT MY FATHER WHO IS IN HEAVEN.
18 I ALSO TELL YOU THAT YOU ARE PETER, AND ON THIS ROCK I WILL BUILD MY ASSEMBLY, AND THE GATES OF HADES WILL NOT PREVAIL AGAINST IT.
19 I WILL GIVE TO YOU THE KEYS OF THE KINGDOM OF HEAVEN, AND WHATEVER YOU BIND ON EARTH WILL HAVE BEEN BOUND IN HEAVEN; AND WHATEVER YOU RELEASE ON EARTH WILL HAVE BEEN RELEASED IN HEAVEN."

Why was Jesus so happy with a statement that seemed so

non profound? A statement that many, including demons, had said of Jesus many times before! Dr. Tim explains that it was not what Peter said that excited Jesus, insomuch that it was the source of what Peter said. Revelation!

Apostles and Prophets flow in revelation, it is this similarity in their offices that makes them such a unique pairing. Apostle Paul puts it well when he says:

GALATIANS 1:11-12
11 BUT I MAKE KNOWN TO YOU, BROTHERS, CONCERNING THE GOOD NEWS WHICH WAS PREACHED BY ME, THAT IT IS NOT ACCORDING TO MAN.
12 FOR NEITHER DID I RECEIVE IT FROM MAN, NOR WAS I TAUGHT IT, BUT IT CAME TO ME THROUGH REVELATION OF JESUS CHRIST.

It is revelation that will make the church a formidable force to the powers of darkness that tout and peddle outdated information. When the church returns back to its apostolic and prophetic roots, God promises that as an institution it will be the last man standing in the earth when the gates of hell come knocking.

The Office of the Prophet predates the gift of prophecy. It even predates the born-again salvation message. This means that you can be called to the office even before you have personally come to the knowledge of Jesus Christ! The office predates your birth let alone your 'birth-again'.

JEREMIAH 1:4-5
4 NOW THE WORD OF THE LORD CAME TO ME, SAYING,

5 "BEFORE I FORMED YOU IN THE BELLY, I KNEW YOU. BEFORE YOU CAME FORTH OUT OF THE WOMB, I SANCTIFIED YOU. I HAVE APPOINTED YOU A PROPHET TO THE NATIONS."

The Office of the Prophet is a decision made on your behalf long before you were born. This is why many say you cannot be ordained into the office because God preordains the Office of the Apostle and the Prophet! For those who say, that was only Old Testament prophets and apostles need to look no further than Galatians where Apostle Paul writes:

GALATIANS 1:15
15 BUT EVEN BEFORE I WAS BORN, GOD CHOSE ME AND CALLED ME BY HIS MARVELLOUS GRACE.

Prophetic officers are called from the womb and therefore it is difficult to discern these officers, but discern we must, if we are ever going to restore them back into the heart of the church and indeed the nation. Without them, the church will go extinct as revelation is the very intention of Jesus as being the builder of the church.

LUKE 1:15
15 FOR HE WILL BE GREAT IN THE SIGHT OF THE LORD, AND HE WILL DRINK NO WINE NOR STRONG DRINK. HE WILL BE FILLED WITH THE HOLY SPIRIT, EVEN FROM HIS MOTHER'S WOMB.

I was five years old when I started having visions. My first vision was in Glasgow, Scotland where my family (five of us) were living in a small flat. I remember looking outside my window and seeing a clear vision of the end times. I saw planes crashing from the sky, the local Ladbrokes demolished as cars crashed into it because the souls of men were being caught up into the sky (what I now know to be the rapture).

I remember hearing a very clear song, I knew then it was angels singing and they sang it so majestically: "Oh when the saints, go marching in, oh when the saints go marching in, I want to be in that number, when the Saints go marching in!"

I remember hearing a sound from Heaven, it would be the first of four times I heard the audible voice of God. He said, "One day you will lead my saints in!"

I always knew I was different, not special, just different. I would have what my teachers called 'day dreams' constantly. My teachers put my visions down to a lack of focus and a need for special after-school care. Visions would consume my mind from a child right up to the age of fifteen when I finally encountered the Lord in a dream. I surrendered my heart to the Lord fully when I was sixteen after hearing His audible voice, for the second time in my life, warn me of a car accident that would have led to our deaths had I not spoken up so my family and I were able to avoid it.

Around 2006, I gave my first national prophecy after a dream I had of a train station called Woolwich Arsenal where I saw violent Muslim men stabbing someone to death and it leading to mass killings throughout London and riots. It was 2011 when London riots broke out and May 2013 when British army soldier Lee Rigby was stabbed in Woolwich by a Muslim extremist. Those who heard the prophecy I had published within many churches in South London began to recognise me as a prophet.

On 9 May 2010, I was invited to Scotland to release a word of the Lord (prophecy) over the United Kingdom by the late and great Bishop Joe Ibojie. As I stood in the pulpit, I had a clear vision that it was necessary that David Cameron would win the elections as the Lord was going to use him to shift the nation out of its stifling alliances. I spoke the word of the Lord and was nearly booed off the stage by upset Scots. Bishop Ibojie explained to me later that Scotland was a SNP (Labour Party leaning) heartland and that people were very upset with my prophecy as Labour had held onto power there for many years. The next day, Scotland woke up to the fact that David Cameron was their new Prime Minister. It was then that churches in Scotland recognised me as a Prophet of the Lord.

Around 2008, I was in the United States when I had a dream. In my dream, I saw the then US Presidential candidate Obama come into a kitchen where I was eating. He barged in and seemed quite rude. He boasted about how he would become the first black president of the United States. I vividly remember not liking him in the dream. I woke up and ignored the dream not knowing what to do with it.

In early 2013, I was in a meeting in Windsor, England when I shared about the health concerns of Madiba (Nelson Mandela). I stood up to a crowd of 500 and shared how Nelson Mandela would pass away later on in the year and that his death would be a significant marker and a dark time for South Africa's politics. In December 2013 Nelson Mandela passed away.

In early 2015, I had a vision in which I saw the United Kingdom's then Prime Minister, David Cameron, jumping off a ship into water with a barrel of treasure in his hand. The Lord spoke to me to prepare Britain to jump ship; to prepare her for an exit from Europe. I spoke this word through social media. When the Brexit vote happened, I was called by the BBC to do an interview on the future of Great Britain. It was from there that God began to raise my profile in the nation as a Prophet of the Lord.

In early 2016, I had a dream in which I saw myself in the same kitchen as I was in in 2013 but this time, the then US Presidential candidate, Donald Trump, entered the kitchen. He calmly knocked on the door and I said "come in". With great respect he sat down and we ate together. In the dream he said to me, "Tomi, can you thank the evangelical church on my behalf for making me the President of the United States of America." I said, "Yes sir, I can". Then I woke up.

I called a friend of mine from Revelation TV and asked if he would interview me. I told him I had a word for the elections. I shared on his program that Donald Trump would be a Cyrus president for the sake of the church and that he would thank the evangelical church for making him President. When it happened, I received a phone call from a United Nations president asking me to come to the United Nations to prophecy over diplomats, UN workers and ambassadors. I accepted the invitation and continue to go each year. It was from there that nations began to recognise me as a Prophet.

In early August 2018, I was invited to Nigeria to raise up the prophetic within the nation. For almost two weeks, we held meetings and training sessions called, 'All May Prophesy'.

During one of those times my Uncle Femi and Aunty Mina Bajomo called me to their house as it was my uncle's birthday. I did not know that I was about to be interviewed in front of his guests, but he proceeded to introduce me to everyone and then put a microphone in my hand to ask me questions.

"So, Tomi, you prophesied Trump's presidency, I saw it on Youtube. What of Nigeria's elections?"

"Uncle, I don't have a word for Nigeria nor have I ever assumed myself Nigeria's prophet", I sheepishly insisted. He replied, "Don't worry, I'll pray for you tonight and God will give you a dream for Nigeria."

That night I had a dream about Nigeria. In my dream I was being brought in front of military officers, but it was what looked like a House of Representatives. I was confused as to why these were military officers and not State politicians. They proceeded to pass judgment on me, but they used Sharia law and not Nigerian law. I woke up and began to publish a word for Nigeria on my Youtube page on a private link. Within five days the prophecy was leaked and went viral. The Nigerian press published it and called me for an interview. It was then that I knew God had raised my profile in Africa.

The Prophetic Office grows on a basis of good stewardship of revelation received. In essence, prophets like any other area of ministry must prove their ministry.

2 TIMOTHY 4:5
5 BUT WATCH THOU IN ALL THINGS, ENDURE AFFLICTIONS, DO THE WORK OF AN EVANGELIST, MAKE FULL PROOF OF THY MINISTRY.

Evangelists that do not win souls are not proving their ministry. Pastors that do not take care of their members are not proving his ministry., Teachers that do not teach are not proving their ministry., Prophet that do not prophesy are not proving their ministry.

I am showing you my track record in the prophetic because I hope by now you can see a word screaming at you as you read through. . . . *RISK!*

A prophet is not a prophet until they can take risks. To carry revelation is not enough unless it is dispensed during the time it still remains a concealed truth. Every revelation is time sensitive and is intended for your elevation! The moment you miss the declaration window between revelation and manifestation you miss the vital elevation God wants to give you! This elevation is important for God's name to be glorified in higher echelons. Knowing you're a prophet is not enough, a nation, a city, a region must receive you as one based on your track record.

1 SAMUEL 3:19-20
19 SAMUEL GREW, AND THE LORD WAS WITH HIM, AND LET NONE OF HIS WORDS FALL TO THE GROUND.
20 ALL ISRAEL FROM DAN EVEN TO BEERSHEBA KNEW THAT SAMUEL WAS ESTABLISHED TO BE A PROPHET OF THE LORD.

GIFT OF PROPHECY	SPIRIT OF PROPHECY	OFFICE OF THE PROPHET
I must be born-again to operate in the gift	I needn't be born-again for the Spirit to be poured out upon me	I am born from the womb to prophecy
Operates within the born-again spirit	Operates upon the world and the church	Operates as a part of who I am
The gift must be stirred up	The Spirit stirs me up	No stirring needed, pure grace
The gift is imparted	The Spirit is poured out	The office is worn (as a mantle)
Within my control	Without my control	Within and without my control
Can be neglected	Can be grieved	Can be false
I work by Him	He works by me	He works through me
Irrevocable	Revocable	Irrevocable
For the church to build the church	For the saved and unsaved to build the world as God intended	For the nation and the church to be built up and transformed into the image God intended
Given by grace	Given because of grace	Pre-given as a gift of grace
Can be dulled	Can be quenched	Cannot be quenched
Is subject to the prophet	Is not subject to the prophet or man	Is subject to the command of the Lord
What you do	How you do it	Who you are
Local	Global	Jurisdictional
Fallible	Infallible	Fallible

4. THE FRIEND OF GOD

The friend of God is in my estimation the greatest achievement of the prophetic and is attainable to all faculties of operation. Believe it or not, man was called friend of God long before there was any salvation package.

ISAIAH 41:8
8 "BUT YOU, ISRAEL, MY SERVANT, JACOB WHOM I HAVE CHOSEN, THE SEED OF ABRAHAM MY FRIEND,

To be counted worthy to become God's friend marked you as a very unique kind of prophet among the faculties of the prophetic. Abraham was called the friend of God long before Jesus died on the Cross. To be called the friend of God is like achieving a place in the prophets' hall of fame. This is not to say that you have arrived, but you are certainly in a place of such unique privilege that information truly only privy to the prophetic officers of the court now gets dispensed to you simply because the King likes you!

God loves everyone! This is a fact. He loves the church and He loves the world. However, as much as God loves everyone, He doesn't like everyone! It is far more powerful to be liked by God than it is to be loved by Him. I know that statement may have shocked some of you, but to be loved of God means that His Son died for you; to be liked by God means that His Son lives for you, with you and in you.

NUMBERS 12:4-8
4 THE LORD SPOKE SUDDENLY TO MOSES, TO AARON, AND TO MIRIAM, "YOU THREE COME OUT TO THE TENT OF MEETING!" THE THREE OF THEM CAME OUT.

5 THE LORD CAME DOWN IN A PILLAR OF CLOUD, AND STOOD AT THE DOOR OF THE TENT, AND CALLED AARON AND MIRIAM; AND THEY BOTH CAME FORWARD.
6 HE SAID, "HEAR NOW MY WORDS. IF THERE IS A PROPHET AMONG YOU, I THE LORD WILL MAKE MYSELF KNOWN TO HIM IN A VISION. I WILL SPEAK WITH HIM IN A DREAM.
7 MY SERVANT MOSES IS NOT SO. HE IS FAITHFUL IN ALL MY HOUSE.
8 WITH HIM I WILL SPEAK MOUTH TO MOUTH, EVEN PLAINLY, AND NOT IN RIDDLES; AND HE SHALL SEE THE LORD'S FORM. WHY THEN WERE YOU NOT AFRAID TO SPEAK AGAINST MY SERVANT, AGAINST MOSES?"

In the Book of Numbers, God makes a clear distinction between prophets and friends. Miriam and Aaron, both being prophets, give a clear warning to Moses about the black woman he had married. What they fail to recognise was that their elitism was trumped by Moses' special status as the friend of God. God loved Miriam, Aaron and Moses equally, but he certainly did not like them equally. Moses was not a man to be messed with and God punished the Prophetess Miriam severely for her assumption. Miriam was a prophet, but Moses was a friend of God!

EXODUS 33:11
11 THE LORD SPOKE TO MOSES FACE TO FACE, AS A MAN SPEAKS TO HIS FRIEND.

Not all prophets are friends, but all friends of God are prophets. It is their special status that grants them not only the ability to hear God, but much more instrumentally, the ability to counsel God and to change God's mind. This privilege is not afforded to any other faculty of the prophetic. Think about it, friends of God have the ability to change the Sovereign's mind.

EXODUS 32:11-14

11 **MOSES BEGGED THE LORD HIS GOD, AND SAID, "THE LORD, WHY DOES YOUR WRATH BURN HOT AGAINST YOUR PEOPLE, THAT YOU HAVE BROUGHT OUT OF THE LAND OF EGYPT WITH GREAT POWER AND WITH A MIGHTY HAND?**
12 **WHY SHOULD THE EGYPTIANS SPEAK, SAYING, 'HE BROUGHT THEM FORTH FOR EVIL, TO KILL THEM IN THE MOUNTAINS, AND TO CONSUME THEM FROM THE SURFACE OF THE EARTH?' TURN FROM YOUR FIERCE WRATH, AND REPENT OF THIS EVIL AGAINST YOUR PEOPLE.**
13 **REMEMBER ABRAHAM, ISAAC, AND ISRAEL, YOUR SERVANTS, TO WHOM YOU SWORE BY YOUR OWN SELF, AND SAID TO THEM, 'I WILL MULTIPLY YOUR SEED AS THE STARS OF THE SKY, AND ALL THIS LAND THAT I HAVE SPOKEN OF I WILL GIVE TO YOUR SEED, AND THEY SHALL INHERIT IT FOREVER.'"**
14 **THE LORD CHANGED HIS MIND OF THE EVIL WHICH HE SAID HE WOULD DO TO HIS PEOPLE.**

Moses changed the mind of God because Moses was not just a prophet, but a friend of God. Being God's friend is a station in the prophetic we all should aspire to! If it was achievable by those of Old who had no covenant with Christ. How much more then by you and I who have a far better covenant than Moses (Hebrews 8:6).

The Biblical definition of a friend is someone who you can share secrets with. Someone who you confide in to tell them what you are about to do. God only shares His secrets with two people!

- His Prophets (Amos 3:7)
- His friends

You may never be a prophet by office, but you can be a friend of God! To be God's friend requires one thing and one thing only, that you fear Him!

PSALM 25:14
14 THE FRIENDSHIP OF THE LORD IS WITH THOSE WHO FEAR HIM. HE WILL SHOW THEM HIS COVENANT.

The truth is, not all prophets fear God. Believe me, as one who has been in the prophetic ministry for over 15 years, I have seen things done in the name of the prophetic that truly have done a disservice to all the faculties of the prophetic and to those called to it.

To fear the Lord is a must for all faculties, but especially those who are to be considered friends of God. To fear God is not the same things as loving God. To truly fear God requires three things of you. A dear father in the Lord, Bishop David Onimisi, taught me this very early in my Christian walk. He calls it the 3 G's you should never mess with:

- God's gold
- God's girls (or guys)
- God's glory

You cannot say you fear God if you don't give to Him extravagantly financially. If your financial commitment to God does not cost you then you may love the Lord, but you certainly do not fear Him. You love the Lord with your obedience, but you honour Him with your giving. Honour is not shown, it is sown!

PROVERBS 3:9
9 HONOUR THE LORD WITH YOUR SUBSTANCE, WITH THE FIRST FRUITS OF ALL YOUR INCREASE:

To fear the Lord means that you are going to honour boundaries with the opposite sex and not give room to the devil. It is only the fear of the Lord that can keep us from crossing this boundary. Finally, we show we fear God when we give Him all the glory and our entire prophetic ministry points back to Him.

Somebody asked me on my Instagram page, "Tomi, you've been on BBC news, you've prophesied over world leaders at the United Nations, you've received powerful words that have changed people's lives, how do you keep the spotlight on Jesus."

My answer to them was this, "To keep the spotlight off of you and on Jesus, you must become the spotlight and shine on Him in every prophecy you give."

Prophets are not immune from hell. We prophets can prophesy in the Name of Jesus and still at the end of it all our future is not secure.

MATTHEW 7:22
22 MANY WILL TELL ME IN THAT DAY, 'LORD, LORD, DIDN'T WE PROPHESY IN YOUR NAME, IN YOUR NAME CAST OUT DEMONS, AND IN YOUR NAME DO MANY MIGHTY WORKS?'

The biggest deception of the prophetic office is to assume, like Miriam, that because God tells you secrets, that He is your friend. We must all, whether by the gift, spirit or office, aspire for the highest faculty of the prophetic. To be the friend of God is to be known by God! It is far greater to be known by God than to know God!

MATTHEW 7:23
24 **THEN I WILL TELL THEM, 'I NEVER KNEW YOU. DEPART FROM ME, YOU WHO WORK INIQUITY.'**

CHAPTER 4 I BUILDING A PROPHETIC LIFESTYLE

TOMI, I WANT TO HEAR GOD?

I get the privilege of travelling all over the world to raise prophets and prophetic people. Everywhere I go I always get asked the same question, "Tomi, "How do I hear God like you do?"

The ability to hear the voice of God lives in every single one of us whether saved or unsaved. The difference is the body of believers should be better equipped to discern the voice of God than the world.

My number one answer to people who want to get better at hearing the voice of God is to build your life around people who are already better than you at hearing the voice of God. They often respond frustratedly, "But Tomi, I listen to audios, I read books and I attend prophetic workshops, how come I am still not where I want to be?"

They often fail to hear my plain speech. If you want to be a little bit prophetic then go to prophetic gatherings, buy audios and indeed read books but if you want to be 'a lot prophetic' then BUILD YOUR ENTIRE LIFE around people who are already better than you at hearing the voice of God.

2 KINGS 6:1-2

1 THE SONS OF THE PROPHETS SAID TO ELISHA, "SEE NOW, THE PLACE WHERE WE MEET BEFORE YOU IS TOO SMALL FOR US.
2 PLEASE LET US GO TO THE JORDAN, AND EVERY MAN TAKE A BEAM FROM THERE, AND LET US MAKE US A PLACE THERE, WHERE WE MAY DWELL." HE ANSWERED, "GO!"

These sons of the prophets (Prophets in Training) said to Elisha the prophet that it wasn't enough to meet with him; they wanted to build houses around him so we could dwell there with him.

There is a price to the prophetic anointing and it is simply not enough to go to a meeting. I often think that people who want to be more prophetic have the wrong ambition. It's just as futile to want to be more prophetic as it is for Eve to be any more like God than she already was. The day you gave your life to Christ you went from being invaded by the Spirit of Prophecy to being invited into the realm of the prophetic where the Spirit lives. Prophetic no longer is just what you do, the prophetic is just as much a vital part of the churches DNA as blood is to the human body. The question is not "which meeting do I go to next", but "how do I build my life around who I am now versus who I was then."

2 CORINTHIANS 5:17

17 THEREFORE IF ANYONE IS IN CHRIST, HE IS A NEW CREATION. THE OLD THINGS HAVE PASSED AWAY. BEHOLD, ALL THINGS HAVE BECOME NEW.

DATING VERSUS MARRIAGE

People often get married with assumptions and preconceived notions of what they are entering into. No doubt influenced by a concoction of how we grew up, conflated with media and Hollywood influence. Those of us who are married are often faced with the stark contrast of the person we met versus the person we married. The person we married demands more from us because we have gone from dating to building our lives together. When you date the prophetic, the prophetic is a nice Sunday addition to a service, it is a one off word you give that really blessed someone and made you feel good for taking the risk. When you marry the prophetic, it requires a lot more of you than a one off word or to make the prophetic an extra tool on your Christian tool belt, because you are building together.

HOW I WENT FROM DATING THE PROPHETIC TO BUILDING WITH THE PROPHETIC

I was sixteen years old when I had my first official girlfriend. Many of you can still remember the complexities of first love. We didn't have WhatsApp or Instagram DM's back then, no, we had MSN Messenger. It was similar to Facebook Messenger only that you had to be behind your dad's desktop computer to use it and wait for the tedious dial up connection just to get access to the internet. Everyday, I would rush home from school to get on MSN messenger so I could talk to the love of my life.

We met through a prayer I made. It sounded a little bit like this

> *Me: "God, I want a girlfriend, I don't want to serve You without one."*
>
> *God: "Okay Tomi, what do you want"*
>
> *Me: "I want her to be a twin (like me). I want her to be the youngest of her twins (like me) and I want her to have blonde hair and blue eyes (unlike me).*
>
> *God: "Hahaha, okay son."*

I have heard God laugh on many occasions, this laughter sounded like the kind of laugh a parent gives when their four-year old son is holding hands with the next door neighbour's daughter.

The next day, I met Katie. She was blonde with blue eyes and dreamy. All the guys wanted her and we never spoke publicly, but her attention was immediately drawn to me. I found out she liked me. You might ask how I found out a girl that I'd never once spoken liked me. She told me on MSN messenger. Yes, everyday at school we would walk past each other and not say a word. Then we would get home frantically to write to each other, "You looked beautiful today."

Like two adolescent star-crossed lovers our public relationship was done in mute, almost like Romeo and Juliet in mime. Our MSN however was as kids today would say, 'lit!!!!' We practically had our whole relationship in text form. I was even happier to find out that not only was she a twin, but she was like me the youngest of her twins.

One morning I had a night vision in which the Lord appeared to me.

God: "Tomi, you asked me for beauty did I give that to you"

Me: "Yes Lord, you did."

God: "Tomi, you asked me for a twin, did I give her to you"

Me: "Yes Lord, you did"

God: "Tomi, you asked me for the youngest twin, did I give it to you"

Me: "Yes Lord, you did!"

God: "Tomi, if Katie were to die today she would die not knowing Me!"

Me: "Oh no! What do I do."

God: "Tell her about My love for her!" Me: "But God, it's 5am!"

God: "She's awake! Go talk to her!"

I woke up from the night vision realising that God was feeding me back my selfish list of aesthetic demands, but that the one thing I had failed to prioritise on the list was her salvation. I went downstairs early that morning and found the love of my life was on MSN Messenger. Here is what the transcript would have looked like that I sent to her:

> Me: "Hey Katie, I know you're awake! Can we talk?"
> Katie: "Hey babe, how did you know I was awake..."

> Me: "God told me..."

> Katie:
> ...
> ...
> ...

> Me: "He told me to come and speak to you..."

> Katie: "Oookay... if God told you to come and speak to me, He should be able to tell you why I'm awake lol."

I reclined on my dad's desktop office chair and asked the Lord to show me what was wrong and why He wanted me to speak to my girlfriend this early in the morning. That's when I had my first vision. I saw an old Kodak film strip and on it were negatives of her life. I saw it so clear that I began to type whilst I was seeing the vision.

Me: Katie, God knows that you were sexually assaulted as a child and that you cried out to him for help, he knows your last boyfriend physically and verbally assaulted you and that somehow you felt as if you deserved it. He knows how much of a secret this has been in your heart that you haven't even shared it with your twin sister. The only person you've shared it with is the school nurse, but God wants you to know He loves you and that He's going to take the pain away of what happened to you.

Me: Katie…. Are you there… Me: Katie!!!

Katie: brb (slang for be right back)

Me: Katie???

Katie: How the f*** did you know all that!

Katie: Bye Tomi!

Tomi: Katie!!!

Auto response: (Katie is not in your contact list)

That was the last time I spoke to Katie, my first ever heart break. You could say Katie never spoke to me again, but on the bright side Katie and I never spoke, period! I was devastated, not because Katie and I broke up but because Katie hardened her heart to an encounter with God. I knew from that day on that I needed to stop dating the prophetic and start building my life around it.

I was eighteen years old when this decision would become a reality to me. Like I wrote earlier, my twin brother and I had planted churches on university campuses all over Britain. Our prophetic ability at the time had developed somewhat, but was still in its infancy. I gave some prophecies that, to this day, I still cringe at. Not because they were false, but because my delivery was not seasoned with the love of God.

I was cocky and arrogant with a gift that I didn't know how to use as anything other than an expository of people's lives. My prophecies unbeknownst to me were very much words of knowledge. We were known as the 'scary twins' on campuses. "Stay away from the scary twins, they know your whole life." I would often marvel at this assumption that we knew everything, this simply wasn't true nevertheless regrettably, we indulged massively in people's assumptions.

1 CORINTHIANS 13:9
9 WE DON'T KNOW EVERYTHING, AND OUR PROPHECIES ARE NOT COMPLETE.

I was invited by a senior pastor and friend of mine to his very large church in North London. He was hosting a prophetic conference and he invited me to come and hear Dr. Sharon Stone speak on the prophetic. Again, as I wrote earlier, I arrived at the meeting to see an extremely tiny woman standing on the pulpit. All of her words and all of her attention pointed people to Jesus! There was no quirky flair, no theatrics, just a tiny lady with a massive heart.

God immediately told me, "That's your mother!" Since then, I attended every meeting she did. When she moved to Windsor England, I moved to Windsor England. I applied for jobs in the area, I made a decision that I wasn't going to date the prophetic any longer, I was going to serve it and build with it. My prophetic grew by association!

1 SAMUEL 10:10-11
10 WHEN THEY CAME THERE TO THE HILL, BEHOLD, A COMPANY OF PROPHETS MET HIM; AND THE SPIRIT OF GOD CAME MIGHTILY ON HIM, AND HE PROPHESIED AMONG THEM.
11 IT HAPPENED, WHEN ALL WHO KNEW HIM BEFORE SAW THAT, BEHOLD, HE PROPHESIED WITH THE PROPHETS, THEN THE PEOPLE SAID ONE TO ANOTHER, "WHAT IS THIS THAT HAS COME TO THE SON OF KISH? IS SAUL ALSO AMONG THE PROPHETS?"

WHEN MEETINGS ARE NOT ENOUGH

Have you ever gone to a prophetic meeting or been in a church where the prophetic is being honoured? It's almost as if within that environment, prophesying is easy. Why? Because honour and the prophetic go hand in hand. You can never experience the prophetic in a church or ministry that does not honour the prophetic.

MARK 6:4-5
4 JESUS SAID TO THEM, "A PROPHET IS NOT WITHOUT HONOUR, EXCEPT IN HIS OWN COUNTRY, AND AMONG HIS OWN RELATIVES, AND IN HIS OWN HOUSE."

5 HE COULD DO NO MIGHTY WORK THERE, EXCEPT THAT HE LAID HIS HANDS ON A FEW SICK PEOPLE, AND HEALED THEM.

When people dishonour the prophetic, the Holy Spirit withdraws. To deny the prophetic is to deny the first nature of the Holy Spirit. People have often said to me that when they come to one of our prophetic meetings it feels like they can only prophecy within the region of the meetings, but that as soon as they go home it all goes away.

The questions took me to task and so I began to study to find an answer why. I knew from the book of 1 Samuel that when Saul prophesied for the first time, it was because he came into the proximity of the prophets, but why did it seem so inconsistent? After all, we want the Holy Spirit to be a part of our everyday lives, hence the title of this book - *Eat, sleep, prophesy, repeat!*

How do we continue to stay in the atmosphere of the Spirit of Prophecy? We think of the gift like a water generator and the Spirit like a river, when the river flows constantly the water generator keeps spinning. In essence, the Spirit of Prophecy and the gift of prophecy make great companions and other than speaking in tongues to stir your gift up, staying in a constant flow of the river of the Holy Spirit through worship will keep your gift stirred. This is why the Holy Spirit is constantly being defined as a river.

JOHN 7:38-39
38 HE WHO BELIEVES IN ME, AS THE SCRIPTURE HAS SAID, FROM WITHIN HIM WILL FLOW RIVERS OF LIVING WATER."

39 BUT HE SAID THIS ABOUT THE SPIRIT, WHICH THOSE BELIEVING IN HIM WERE TO RECEIVE. FOR THE HOLY SPIRIT WAS NOT YET GIVEN, BECAUSE JESUS WASN'T YET GLORIFIED.

The question for those of you who want a constant prophetic flow is how do I keep the river flowing?

In Numbers 11:14, Moses becomes tired of the amount of people coming to him for a prophecy. He has literally fallen into the pitfalls of the prophetic and has set himself up to be everybody's guru and link to the Father. He complains to God because when you build your ministry on a one prophet pyramid, your plan soon becomes unsustainable. I call this *the need to be needed!* It is a very dangerous place for prophetic people to be not to mention detrimental to health and dangerous.

God responds to Moses by telling him:

NUMBERS 11:16-17
16 ..."GATHER TO ME SEVENTY MEN OF THE ELDERS OF ISRAEL, WHOM YOU KNOW TO BE THE ELDERS OF THE PEOPLE, AND OFFICERS OVER THEM; AND BRING THEM TO THE TENT OF MEETING, THAT THEY MAY STAND THERE WITH YOU.
17 I WILL COME DOWN AND TALK WITH YOU THERE. I WILL TAKE OF THE SPIRIT WHICH IS ON YOU, AND WILL PUT IT ON THEM; AND THEY SHALL BEAR THE BURDEN OF THE PEOPLE WITH YOU, THAT YOU NOT BEAR IT YOURSELF ALONE.

Moses gathers 70 elders together and calls them to a prophetic meeting. Just by proximity alone, God takes of the Spirit of Prophecy that is upon Moses and pours His power out on the seventy elders. This is what sharing the burden looked like in the local church of Moses:

NUMBERS 11:25
25 THE LORD CAME DOWN IN THE CLOUD, AND SPOKE TO HIM, AND TOOK OF THE SPIRIT THAT WAS ON HIM, AND PUT IT ON THE SEVENTY ELDERS: AND IT HAPPENED THAT WHEN THE SPIRIT RESTED ON THEM, THEY PROPHESIED, BUT THEY DID SO NO MORE.

The Spirit of God came down into the meeting and the seventy elders began to prophesy and just at the moment of Moses' greatest jubilation, the tap stopped running and those seventy elders in the prophetic meeting never prophesied again. What a disappointment these elders must have felt. As long as they were in the meeting they could prophesy, but as soon as they left the tent where the meeting was being held, the Bible says that they could not prophecy again. This Chapter then goes on to reveal something that for many years was very confusing to me.

NUMBERS 11:26
26 HOWEVER, TWO MEN, WHOSE NAMES WERE ELDAD AND MEDAD, HAD REMAINED IN THE CAMP. THEY WERE LISTED AMONG THE ELDERS, BUT DID NOT GO OUT TO THE TENT. YET THE SPIRIT ALSO RESTED ON THEM, AND THEY PROPHESIED IN THE CAMP. A YOUNG MAN RAN AND TOLD MOSES, "ELDAD AND MEDAD ARE PROPHESYING IN THE CAMP."

Eldad and Medad are two characters that confounded me for years. They are the perfect picture of those two members in every church that never shows up to any of the meetings. They pray for prophetic gatherings to be launched in their local church and finally Pastor Moses puts a special impartation service on and they register, but they don't show up. Every pastor reading this book right now is sighing in suspended disbelief and consoling camaraderie!

How is it that these two men could register for the meeting, not show up and yet in the camp they could prophecy. It seems almost as if the Holy Spirit is condoning rebellion at most, apathy at least in allowing these two to benefit from the reward of those who actually bothered to turn up to the meeting.

I ignored this Scripture for many years in my prophetic training as I didn't want to teach people that the secret to prophesying outside the prophetic meetings is to never show up to a prophetic meeting. One day, Mum Sharon asked me to teach on Prophetic Discipleship. The Holy Spirit led me back to this very chapter and gave me the answer to years of groaning in the Spirit, searching for one. I said,

"Lord it's not fair that seventy people can show up to a meeting and you allow your Holy Spirit to touch them and they prophesy once and then relegate flow consistently through two people that registered but didn't even bother to show up to the meeting, but instead stayed in the camp."

Then the Lord said, *"Tomi, you can come to every meeting and never be connected to the camp!"*

That was it! Such a simple word carried on the breath of the Holy Spirit into my spiritual ears ceased years of agonising searching and confusion. The Holy Spirit doesn't pick people the way we do! When we select those worthy of eldership, we look for the oldest, the ones that show up, the ones that offer good eye service but the Holy Spirit isn't looking for people content with coming to the prophetic meeting, He is looking for people who are connected to the prophetic camp.

A meeting means you're going home, a camp means that you're so connected to the prophetic that you want to eat, sleep, prophesy, repeat! A meeting means that the prophetic is another tool you want to add to your tool belt. A camp means that you are building your life, raising your kids, having breakfast, lunch and dinner wherever the prophetic is. A meeting means that you dictate how much you are willing to give and how far you are willing to journey. A camp means that your home is mobile and that your life is flexible and depends entirely on where the Holy Spirit wants to go. The seventy elders were content with a prophetic meeting, but Eldad and Medad were not looking for a prophetic top up, they wanted to bask in the vicinity of the prophetic. They didn't just want to drink from the waters, they wanted to live in the waters.

For those who want the Holy Spirit to find them wherever they are, it is not enough to go to the meetings, the question is, what is your prophetic camp?

MEETING MENTALITY	CAMP MENTALITY
Prophetic as a tool on the tool belt	Prophetic is my DNA
Prophesy to me	Prophesy through me
Drink from the flow	Live in the flow
Moment	Lifestyle
I accommodate the prophetic as part of my life	The prophetic accommodates me as part of His life
I come to get stirred up for the moment	I stay stirred up in every moment
I want to be blessed and be a blessing to others	I want to build and be a builder of others
Enable me	Empower me
Mentor me	Adopt me
Inform me	Transform me
Speak to me here	Speak to me everywhere
Where I go	Where I grow
Retreat	Reside
Show up	Sow up
Fellowship	Community

IN SUMMARY

If you want to transfer from meeting mentality to camp mentality, there are five essential things you and I must do.

1. Meditation
Build your entire life by the river by lifestyle meditation (Psalm 1:2, Joshua1:8)

90

2. Proximity

Be around people who prophesy more than you. Discipleship without proximity is merely a fan club. Scripture shows that those truly hungry for the prophetic were willing to build their lives and houses around prophetic people. (2 Kings 6:2, 1 Samuel 10:5, 1 Samuel10:10)

3. Honour

Excellently service those whose office and gift are where you want to be (Mark 6:4, 1 Kings 19:21.)

4. Community

Join a prophetic community. It's not enough to go to a meeting you must be connected to a camp. (Numbers 11)

5. Build

Be committed to building the prophetic camps and communities (2 Kings 6:1-2)

TER 5 | MY SHEEP HEAR MY VOICE

WHAT DOES GOD SOUND LIKE?

The number one question I always get asked is "Tomi, will you prophesy to me?" The number two question I always get asked is, "What does God sound like!" I prefer question two because it takes a body of people from a mentality of enablement to empowerment. Jesus points out the ultimate goal of the five-fold ministry gifts in Ephesians 4 as being to equip the saints for the work of the ministry.

EPHESIANS 4:11-12
11 HE GAVE SOME TO BE APOSTLES; AND SOME, PROPHETS; AND SOME, EVANGELISTS; AND SOME, SHEPHERDS AND TEACHERS;
12 FOR THE EQUIPPING OF THE SAINTS, TO THE WORK OF THE MINISTRY, TO THE BUILDING UP OF THE BODY OF CHRIST;

We are called as prophetic people not only to bless people and nations through the voice of God. We are called to empower God's people to hear God's voice. In the New Testament ,all the saints get access to the voice of God.

JOHN 10:27
27 MY SHEEP HEAR MY VOICE, AND I KNOW THEM, AND THEY FOLLOW ME.

Hearing the voice of God is no longer exclusive to the

Prophets or the governing ecclesiology of your local church, hearing God's voice is open to every single saint in the church who professes Christ as their shepherd. That means, we all get to have an Eden experience with the Lord that is daily and tangible.

THE WORST THING THAT CAN HAPPEN TO A CHURCH

I have been in ministry for half of my life and, in my years of ministry, I have seen churches split, pastors control their flock through fear, pastors ousted for sexual misdeeds, leaders arrested for mismanagement of church funds and pastors and prophets who served God honourably having premature deaths. I have lost great friends in the ministry to heart attacks, pulmonary embolisms and the like. Nothing has prepared me to see the day nor prepare the sermon where evil things happen to both good and bad actors in the church. These are often defined as the death blows to any church and especially when such incidences happen around or indeed through spiritual leaders.

However, all of this is nothing compared with God's judgment upon the churches in nations. For we can all agree that whilst these incidences are tragic, devastating and disappointing, they are not the worst thing that can happen to a living church. I have seen churches move on past all of these things to seemingly thrive (at least according to man's estimates).

The worst thing that can ever happen to a living church is for it to lose its lamp stand.

4 BUT I HAVE THIS AGAINST YOU, THAT YOU LEFT YOUR FIRST LOVE.
5 REMEMBER THEREFORE FROM WHERE YOU HAVE FALLEN, AND REPENT AND DO THE FIRST WORKS; OR ELSE I AM COMING TO YOU SWIFTLY, AND WILL MOVE YOUR LAMP STAND OUT OF ITS PLACE, UNLESS YOU REPENT.

A church that loses its lamp stand is no longer a church, it's a social gathering. The lamp stand represents the illumination of prophetic insight and revelation that makes the institution of the church the bright beacon it is in the earth today. I implore churches all over the world that you can lose your building, your quarterly budget, your charity status, your speakers, your microphones, your keyboardist, your worship leader, you can even lose your pastor and survive but at, all costs, you must preserve your lamp stand!

When churches lose their lamp stand, they enter into a dark age, leaving the world to light the way. Samuel was called at the final hour just before the lamp of God went out, God in His infinite mercy, raised up a prophet.

1 SAMUEL 3:3-4
3 AND THE LAMP OF GOD HADN'T YET GONE OUT, AND SAMUEL HAD LAID DOWN IN THE LORD'S TEMPLE, WHERE THE ARK OF GOD WAS;
4 THAT THE LORD CALLED SAMUEL; AND HE SAID, "HERE I AM."

When the lamp goes out, the world has no light because the church can no longer see on its behalf. When the lamp goes out, the voice of Christ and the voice of the Church become irrelevant in national affairs.

REVELATION 18:23

23 THE LIGHT OF A LAMP WILL SHINE NO MORE AT ALL IN YOU. THE VOICE OF THE BRIDEGROOM AND OF THE BRIDE WILL BE HEARD NO MORE AT ALL IN YOU; FOR YOUR MERCHANTS WERE THE PRINCES OF THE EARTH; FOR WITH YOUR SORCERY ALL THE NATIONS WERE DECEIVED.

For there is yet hope in a nation as long as the lamp of prophecy and revelation is burning bright in every church and it is the mission of this book to restore the lamp stands back into the church. For how can we come to the house of God and never hear from the God of the house? We must have a heart to see the gifts of the Spirit returned back to the church, but especially that *ALL MAY PROPHESY!*

1 CORINTHIANS 14:1

1 FOLLOW AFTER LOVE, AND EARNESTLY DESIRE SPIRITUAL GIFTS, BUT ESPECIALLY THAT YOU MAY PROPHESY.

In these dark times, I believe that God is going to grow the church in the nations and many will flock into the house of God. It will not happen because of a special training on how to grow your church, but because of prophetic encounters. The church will be built up because the Spirit of Prophecy is being given permission again to breath new oxygen into our church organisms. This will mark a time of refreshing for those in the Body of Christ that accept it, for the Lord will bring about supernatural church growth through those willing to participate in facilitating the Spirit of Prophecy in their services again.

4 THE PERSON WHO SPEAKS IN A FOREIGN LANGUAGE BUILDS HIMSELF UP, BUT THE PERSON WHO PROPHESIES BUILDS UP THE CHURCH.

GOD'S VOICE IS NOT HEARD, GOD'S VOICE IS DISCERNED

For those of you struggling to hear the voice of God, your struggle is shared by the masses of people who also participate in the same effort. One day I was in a private mentoring group with Mum Sharon when she said this, 'The voice of God is not heard, the voice of God is discerned.'

That statement has lived with me ever since and has become the foundation upon which I raise prophets all over the world. The truth is, we don't hear God's voice, we simply become better at discerning the voice of a God who is speaking to us all the time. I am not talking about discernment as a gift of the Spirit (even though it sure is helpful to have it) I am talking about the natural discernment of the supernatural spirit within man.

Paul in 1 Corinthians 2 says:

1 CORINTHIANS 2:9-12
**9 "THINGS WHICH AN EYE DIDN'T SEE, AND AN EAR DIDN'T HEAR, WHICH DIDN'T ENTER INTO THE HEART OF MAN, THESE GOD HAS PREPARED FOR THOSE WHO LOVE HIM."
10 BUT TO US, GOD REVEALED THEM THROUGH THE SPIRIT. FOR THE SPIRIT SEARCHES ALL THINGS, YES, THE DEEP THINGS OF GOD.**

11 FOR WHO AMONG MEN KNOWS THE THINGS OF A MAN, EXCEPT THE SPIRIT OF THE MAN, WHICH IS IN HIM? EVEN SO, NO ONE KNOWS THE THINGS OF GOD, EXCEPT GOD'S SPIRIT. 12 BUT WE RECEIVED, NOT THE SPIRIT OF THE WORLD, BUT THE SPIRIT WHICH IS FROM GOD, THAT WE MIGHT KNOW THE THINGS THAT WERE FREELY GIVEN TO US BY GOD.

So we already see, God does not appeal to natural ears, natural eyes or natural hearts, but He reveals to spiritual eyes, spiritual ears and spiritual hearts. Revelation is God's spirit communicating with our human spirit. This communication is uploaded onto our natural output monitors of our mind in the form of pictures or images.

Our human spirit is the CPU (central processing unit) of revelation, but it is also the CPU of our own human thoughts and demonic thoughts imposed on us from the spirit of the world (governed by Satan). So revelation is competing in the information highway of our minds. Our spirits get to be the processor of truth versus lies. Our human spirit has the capacity to sift through human and demonic interference passing through our senses to capture the voice of God. However, we must exercise our spiritual capacity to discern the Holy Spirit revealing truth versus the enemy trying to pass facts or truthful statements as statements of truth.

1 CORINTHIANS 2:14-15
15 NOW THE NATURAL MAN DOESN'T RECEIVE THE THINGS OF GOD'S SPIRIT, FOR THEY ARE FOOLISHNESS TO HIM, AND HE CAN'T KNOW THEM, BECAUSE THEY ARE SPIRITUALLY DISCERNED. 15 BUT HE WHO IS SPIRITUAL DISCERNS ALL THINGS, AND HE HIMSELF IS JUDGED BY NO ONE.

The carnally minded man does not take hold of spiritual things because he regards it as just 'day dreaming' or 'crazy dreams', and so dismisses it. The spiritual man sits down and with his own CPU (his spirit) scans his thoughts and senses to discern whether this was God, the flesh or the devil. This requires work, which unfortunately few are willing to do and very few are willing to accept that we live in a fallible world where it is possible to be wrong, even where there is common consensus among the prophetic (See 2 Chronicles 18) as a case study.

The Spirit of Prophecy can never be wrong, but the prophet can be! The prophetic is infallible but whether gift or office, the prophet is fallible. This is why prophets need to be humble like Moses because knowledge will puff you up. (1 Corinthians 8:1)

WHEN WAS THE LAST TIME YOU EXERCISED YOUR SPIRIT?

The human spirit surrendered to the Holy Spirit and properly exercised becomes a truth scanner that surveys the spiritual terrain for possible misstatements or errors. It becomes a well-trained traffic warden, sifting through the daily mental minutia for what is of God and filtering out what is not of God. However, your human spirit needs exercise, otherwise it becomes lazy!

HEBREWS 5:14
14 BUT SOLID FOOD IS FOR THOSE WHO ARE FULL GROWN, WHO BY REASON OF USE HAVE THEIR SENSES EXERCISED TO DISCERN GOOD AND EVIL.

Discernment is like meditation, prayer and fasting; it is a daily spiritual exercise.

Several years ago my brother pastored a thriving church in Northampton, United Kingdom. His treasurer back then had reported that a large sum of the church's money had been stolen from her house. She noticed when she was about to take it to the bank to be cashed in. My brother called me to come the three hour jouney up to Northampton to see him.

I sat in his office and saw he was very distressed, I asked him what was wrong. He proceeded to explain the reason he called me up. He asked if I could pray with him and ask God who stole the church finances. We both prayed together in his office that day and we both saw a picture of the same girl at the same time. This was a lovely girl and a new convert so we knew nothing about her. However, there was a feeling surrounding this mental picture. Some of you would call it 'a gut feeling'.

We just felt strongly that this new convert was responsible for stealing this offering. So we discussed the best way to confront her and what our possible exit strategy was if we were wrong. My brother decided that since he was the pastor that it would be best if I called her to a private meeting and confronted her.

I called her into my brothers office and she said, "Hi, Apostle Tomi, I've heard so much about you!" My first statement was, "You did it, didn't you?"
Immediately she recoiled and began to shake, her eyes filled

with water as her composure broke and sheepishly she responded, "Yes."

What was that? That was the twin brothers exercising the discernment of their spirit (surrendered to the Holy Spirit) concerning a mental picture that they had both received after enquiring of the Lord. When we saw this mental picture it was revealed to our sense of sight, then it was confirmed with our sense of feeling (or gut feeling), but you see, our senses were trying to sift out whether it was God or whether it was the accuser of the brethren (Satan) speaking to us trying to hurt our relationship with a new convert. Can you imagine if Day One of this girl's salvation was to face accusation from a spiritual leader? What a wounding that would have been to her! We had no prior knowledge of the girl's background, we just knew that it was her.

Well, Tomi what happened to her? We made sure she repaid the money and then we loved her back into the will of God for her life!

You see, discerning takes the exercise of your human spirit (again a caveat being that your human spirit is surrendered to the Holy Spirit) but even the unsaved can discern with their unregenerate human spirit, how much more the spiritual church who's spirits have been revived by the Holy Spirit.

PROVERBS 16:32
32 ONE WHO IS SLOW TO ANGER IS BETTER THAN THE MIGHTY; ONE WHO RULES HIS SPIRIT, THAN HE WHO TAKES A CITY.

You have to take responsibility for your own spiritual training.

When Paul is speaking about the senses, he is speaking about:

- Sight
- Sound
- Smell
- Touch
- Taste

These are not just natural senses but spiritual ones as well. The Bible is filled with people who see, hear, smell, touch and even taste in the spirit.

SPIRITUAL SENSE	SCRIPTURE REFERENCE
SIGHT	Revelation 15:1, Jeremiah 1:11, Amos 7:8, Jeremiah 33:3
SOUND	Ezekiel 10:13, 1 Samuel 3:10,
SMELL	Psalm 115:6, 1 Corinthians 12:17, Song of Songs 7:7, Psalm 45:8
TASTE	Psalm 119:103, Ezekiel 3:1-3, Revelation 10:9-10, Psalm 34:8
TOUCH	Isaiah 6:7, 1 Samuel 10:26,

THE DANGER OF NOT HAVING ALL YOUR SENSES EXERCISED

There are many books that help believers find their area of specialisation in the prophetic. We have names for the two most common ones, nabi and roeh. These are two Hebrew words taken from the Book of Samuel.

1 SAMUEL 9:9
9 (IN EARLIER TIMES IN ISRAEL, WHEN A MAN WENT TO INQUIRE OF GOD, THUS HE SAID, "COME, AND LET US GO TO THE SEER"; FOR HE WHO IS NOW CALLED A PROPHET (NABI) WAS BEFORE CALLED A SEER (ROEH).)

NABI

A nabi prophet is often described as a bubbling brook prophet or inspired one and usually hears more than they see.

A roeh typically receives from dreams, visions and special encounters.

Whilst I celebrate how far the Prophetic has come to create terminology that gives us a map to navigate its vast terrain, I don't believe that the Lord intended for prophetic people to remain glued to one particular way of receiving from Him. I believe there are people more equipped in one area of receiving from God than in another but I believe more deeply, that God will find every way to communicate with us using all our senses the more we exercise them and engage with His Holy Spirit.

I actually believe that those of us who have been practicing are in a great season of promotion surrounding the prophetic and that God is going to release such lifestyle prophetic that it will be like Adam and God walking in the garden in the cool of the day. That what we commonly call the prophetic will become the public overflow of our personal relationship with the Father through His indwelling Holy Spirit.

There is a great coming danger and it is coming to the Body of Christ. Indeed it is already here! It is a deception so great that it can even deceive God's elect! It is going to come in the form of false Messiah's and false Prophets!

MATTHEW 24:24
24 **FOR THERE WILL ARISE FALSE MESSIAHS, AND FALSE PROPHETS, AND THEY WILL SHOW GREAT SIGNS AND WONDERS, SO AS TO LEAD ASTRAY, IF POSSIBLE, EVEN THE CHOSEN ONES.**

No wonder the church has by and large kicked out the prophets, they are collateral damage in the safe guarding of the flock of Christ. It's unfortunate that genuine prophets get mixed up in a bag of false ones and those with a Messiah complex get confused with those who carry the Messiah's heart, but the Bible is clear that this is a present and coming danger. So I understand why pastors have been suspicious around this area of ministry because there is no tangible litmus test to differentiate true prophets from false prophets.

The only thing we can truly do, is become far more superior at discerning falsehood than we have ever been in our lives. Sorry pastors, but it's a 'discern or discriminate' world! Once we discriminate, we erode at the very DNA of the church which is a hub for revelation and prophetic communication and our churches become empty vessels of recycled and regurgitated truths. To accurately discern we must move into prophetic trainings that have all our senses trained. The best example I can draw of this is in the Book of Genesis 27.

Isaac's natural senses had diminished, he was blind and old when he was meant to bless Esau but mistakenly blessed his twin brother Jacob who managed to deceive him. The first sense that Isaac relied upon was touch!

GENESIS 27:21
21 **ISAAC SAID TO JACOB, "PLEASE COME NEAR, THAT I MAY FEEL YOU, MY SON, WHETHER YOU ARE REALLY MY SON ESAU OR NOT."**

Isaac knew that Esau was hairy and Jacob was not at all but Jacob on the advice of his mother went and got sheep wool and put it on his arms.

GENESIS 27:23
23 **AND HE DISCERNED HIM NOT, BECAUSE HIS HANDS WERE HAIRY, AS HIS BROTHER ESAU'S HANDS: SO HE BLESSED HIM.**

The second sense Isaac relied on was the voice.

GENESIS 27:22
22 **JACOB WENT NEAR TO ISAAC HIS FATHER. HE FELT HIM, AND SAID, "THE VOICE IS JACOB'S VOICE, BUT THE HANDS ARE THE HANDS OF ESAU."**

In other words, Jacob was saying, this feels like God it just doesn't sound like God! The third sense Jacob relied on was taste!

GENESIS 27:24-25
24 HE SAID, "ARE YOU REALLY MY SON ESAU?" HE SAID, "I AM."
25 HE SAID, "BRING IT NEAR TO ME, AND I WILL EAT OF MY SON'S VENISON, THAT MY SOUL MAY BLESS YOU." HE BROUGHT IT NEAR TO HIM, AND HE ATE. HE BROUGHT HIM WINE, AND HE DRANK.

Isaac knew how his son's food tasted! This food was made to taste exactly the same as Esau's food.

The fourth sense Jacob relied on was smell

GENESIS 27:26-27
26 HIS FATHER ISAAC SAID TO HIM, "COME NEAR NOW, AND KISS ME, MY SON."
27 HE CAME NEAR, AND KISSED HIM. HE SMELLED THE SMELL OF HIS CLOTHING, AND BLESSED HIM, AND SAID, "BEHOLD, THE SMELL OF MY SON IS AS THE SMELL OF A FIELD WHICH THE LORD HAS BLESSED.

Jacob had four of his senses exercised to discern whether this was indeed Esau or his deceitful son Jacob. The only sense that let him down was his sight!

GENESIS 27:1
1 IT HAPPENED, THAT WHEN ISAAC WAS OLD, AND HIS EYES WERE DIM, SO THAT HE COULD NOT SEE, HE CALLED ESAU HIS ELDER SON, AND SAID TO HIM, "MY SON?" HE SAID TO HIM, "HERE I AM."

FROM SEEKER SENSITIVE TO SENSITIVE SEEKERS

One of the greatest dangers the prophetic is coming into is that the devil has found a way to sound like God, smell like God, taste like God, feel like God and look like God and unless we train the church to engage all their senses in discerning good and evil, it is highly possible to be deceived. God is getting ready to take the church from being 'seeker sensitive' to being 'sensitive seekers.'

All senses being trained doesn't mean that it has to be one person fully sensitised to the Holy Spirit, but it does mean that the Body of Christ has got to learn to see itself as an organism compiling of different spiritual sensory anatomies. That when each organ works together and celebrates its prophetic diversity, it becomes a singular and unbeatable organism in the hand of God.

1 CORINTHIANS 12:14-21
14 **FOR THE BODY IS NOT ONE MEMBER, BUT MANY.**
15 **IF THE FOOT WOULD SAY, "BECAUSE I'M NOT THE HAND, I'M NOT PART OF THE BODY," IT IS NOT THEREFORE NOT PART OF THE BODY.**
16 **IF THE EAR WOULD SAY, "BECAUSE I'M NOT THE EYE, I'M NOT PART OF THE BODY," IT'S NOT THEREFORE NOT PART OF THE BODY.**
17 **IF THE WHOLE BODY WERE AN EYE, WHERE WOULD THE HEARING BE? IF THE WHOLE WERE HEARING, WHERE WOULD THE SMELLING BE?**
18 **BUT NOW GOD HAS SET THE MEMBERS, EACH ONE OF THEM, IN THE BODY, JUST AS HE DESIRED.**
19 **IF THEY WERE ALL ONE MEMBER, WHERE WOULD THE BODY BE?**

20 BUT NOW THEY ARE MANY MEMBERS, BUT ONE BODY. 21 THE EYE CAN'T TELL THE HAND, "I HAVE NO NEED FOR YOU," OR AGAIN THE HEAD TO THE FEET, "I HAVE NO NEED FOR YOU."

The church is a giant sensory organism, intended by God to be corporately spiritually sensitive in the pursuit of discerning God in a vast spiritual terrain. When we learn to stop seeing ourselves as a denomination and start seeing ourselves as an organ within a body, we will unify not out of compulsion, but out of necessity!

1 CORINTHIANS 12:26-27
26 WHEN ONE MEMBER SUFFERS, ALL THE MEMBERS SUFFER WITH IT. OR WHEN ONE MEMBER IS HONOURED, ALL THE MEMBERS REJOICE WITH IT. 27 NOW YOU ARE THE BODY OF CHRIST, AND MEMBERS INDIVIDUALLY.

TRUTHFULLY STATED VERSUS STATEMENTS OF TRUTH

We have just heard that Satan like Jacob to Esau can mimic God's signature and that it is possible to receive as God what is not of God. A lot of spiritual leaders will encourage us to just stick with the written word of God. Whilst this is one sure way to discern the voice of God, Satan is the perfect mocking bird (a bird that can mimic the songs of other birds and insects). He is the father of all lies, but not in the obtrusive way we might think.

JOHN 8:44

44 YOU ARE OF YOUR FATHER, THE DEVIL, AND YOU WANT TO DO THE DESIRES OF YOUR FATHER. HE WAS A MURDERER FROM THE BEGINNING, AND DOESN'T STAND IN THE TRUTH, BECAUSE THERE IS NO TRUTH IN HIM. WHEN HE SPEAKS A LIE, HE SPEAKS ON HIS OWN; FOR HE IS A LIAR, AND ITS FATHER.

What makes Satan the father of lies is his ability to masterfully present statements of truth and traffic them as truthful statements! He has been doing this for Centuries in churches, marriages, families and nations from the beginning of time. When Satan came to tempt Jesus, He did not come as a Hollywood snake. He came to Jesus presenting Himself as the voice of God, even quoting Scripture!

LUKE 4:9-11

9 HE LED HIM TO JERUSALEM, AND SET HIM ON THE PINNACLE OF THE TEMPLE, AND SAID TO HIM, "IF YOU ARE THE SON OF GOD, CAST YOURSELF DOWN FROM HERE, 10 FOR IT IS WRITTEN, 'HE WILL PUT HIS ANGELS IN CHARGE OF YOU, TO GUARD YOU;' 11 AND, 'ON THEIR HANDS THEY WILL BEAR YOU UP, LEST PERHAPS YOU DASH YOUR FOOT AGAINST A STONE.'"

He quotes Psalm 91 to Jesus. This is a classic example of a statement of truth not being truthfully stated. It was taken out of its context to suit satan's purpose. I've got news for you! Satan reads the Bible and knows each verse off by heart. The church can only be safe from the devil for so long by hiding behind the Scripture before we realise that we must be Scriptural and spiritual at the same time!

2 CORINTHIANS 3:6

6 WHO ALSO MADE US SUFFICIENT AS SERVANTS OF A NEW COVENANT; NOT OF THE LETTER, BUT OF THE SPIRIT. FOR THE LETTER KILLS, BUT THE SPIRIT GIVES LIFE.

We must not be afraid to venture into the Spirit if we are going to get to the truth because Satan can traffic statements of truth to deceive the elect. Without the Holy Spirit the Bible is content without context. The Holy Spirit is the One who guides us into all truth and so without Him we become prey to an enemy who weaponises Scriptural truths to deceive us!

JOHN 16:13

13 HOWEVER WHEN HE, THE SPIRIT OF TRUTH, HAS COME, HE WILL GUIDE YOU INTO ALL TRUTH, FOR HE WILL NOT SPEAK FROM HIMSELF; BUT WHATEVER HE HEARS, HE WILL SPEAK. HE WILL DECLARE TO YOU THINGS THAT ARE COMING.

Satan has upped his strategy against the church and, like Jacob, is disguising himself as God's messenger so that he can deceive us.

2 CORINTHIANS 11:14

14 AND NO WONDER, FOR EVEN SATAN DISGUISES AS AN ANGEL OF LIGHT.

The prophetic is no longer optional. It must become our lifestyle again if we are ever going to see nations transformed into the image of Christ.

,UWING YOUR DISCERNMENT

Discernment is more than a gut feeling. Discernment is a recognition to one, or more than one, sense that God is revealing Himself to you! There are four things you and I can do daily to grow our level of discernment.

1. INVESTIGATE EVERYTHING, ASSUME NOTHING

Be a master investigator. Learn to ask your spirit the right questions!

1 CORINTHIANS 2:15
15 BUT HE WHO IS SPIRITUAL DISCERNS ALL THINGS, AND HE HIMSELF IS JUDGED BY NO ONE.

Don't be a 'God said to me' Christian. Don't accept things as God straight away. Sooner or later you will lose all credibility because you haven't used your powers of investigation.

Give every vision, dream and voice the assumption of innocence, but also prove it innocent as well. Discern all things! Don't assume that something isn't God, but neither assume that everything is God. Some things are just the cheese you ate last night. Allow your spirit to become a filter system for good and evil.

There are some visions, some dreams and some moments where God speaks that, if you don't investigate the encounter for fear or assumption, it will end the spiritual encounter!

EXODUS 3:1-4

**1 NOW MOSES WAS KEEPING THE FLOCK OF JETHRO, HIS FATHER-IN-LAW, THE PRIEST OF MIDIAN, AND HE LED THE FLOCK TO THE BACK OF THE WILDERNESS, AND CAME TO GOD'S MOUNTAIN, TO HOREB.
2 THE ANGEL OF THE LORD APPEARED TO HIM IN A FLAME OF FIRE OUT OF THE MIDST OF A BUSH. HE LOOKED, AND BEHOLD, THE BUSH BURNED WITH FIRE, AND THE BUSH WAS NOT CONSUMED.
3 MOSES SAID, "I WILL TURN ASIDE NOW, AND SEE THIS GREAT SIGHT, WHY THE BUSH IS NOT BURNT."
4 WHEN THE LORD SAW THAT HE TURNED ASIDE TO SEE, GOD CALLED TO HIM OUT OF THE MIDST OF THE BUSH, AND SAID, "MOSES! MOSES!" HE SAID, "HERE I AM."**

Moses decided to investigate. If he had decided that he was hallucinating or that he was suffering altitude sickness, he would have missed his calling! God will always reveal himself to one of your spiritual senses first, but then, if you don't turn to investigate the encounter you may miss it!

2. DON'T LEAN ON YOUR OWN UNDERSTANDING, BUT ACKNOWLEDGE GOD IN EVERYTHING

When God reveals something to one of your senses, He is often always inviting your other senses into the encounter. It is not enough to just see, engaging your other senses will help you better discern what the Lord is showing you. When God gave Jeremiah a vision He said:

JEREMIAH 1:11

11 MOREOVER THE WORD OF THE LORD CAME TO ME, SAYING, "JEREMIAH, WHAT DO YOU SEE?" I SAID, "I SEE A BRANCH OF AN ALMOND TREE."

Jeremiah saw a branch of an almond tree. Now notice, he didn't go out and prophesy over someone that they are God's precious little almond. He leaned on what He was hearing to explain a vision that he initially could not understand.

JEREMIAH 1:12
12 THEN THE LORD SAID TO ME, "YOU HAVE SEEN WELL; FOR I WATCH OVER MY WORD TO PERFORM IT."

Two senses are cooperating to give a fuller understanding of what the Lord is revealing to Jeremiah. What if God were to show you a vision of a dog? If you were to lean on your own understanding, I'd bet that your interpretation of the vision will depend largely on your view towards dogs. People with a negative experience of dogs often equate them with being bad things, but people who have grown up with dogs equate them to be good things. Immerse yourself in the encounter you are having with the Lord and let Him reveal Himself to you.

3. DON'T DULL YOUR SPIRITUAL SENSES

There are things that we can do to dull or indeed sharpen our spiritual senses. In fact, when Adam's physical senses were opened, his spiritual senses were shut down.

GENESIS 3:7
7 THE EYES OF BOTH OF THEM WERE OPENED, AND THEY KNEW THAT THEY WERE NAKED. THEY SEWED FIG LEAVES TOGETHER, AND MADE THEMSELVES APRONS.

Your body has senses and so does your spirit. Your spirit has a sense of taste, touch, sight, smell and hearing just like your body does. Your spirit has eyes, ears, taste buds, a nose and all the faculties disposed to the body are part of the spiritual make up.

The realm that you are most sensitive to will determine the realm that you live in. Just like physical senses report back to the brain from the central nervous system, spiritual senses report back to the spiritual mind which must be renewed daily so that we can actively receive and transmit from the spirit.

EPHESIANS 4:22-24
22 THAT YOU PUT AWAY, AS CONCERNING YOUR FORMER WAY OF LIFE, THE OLD MAN, THAT GROWS CORRUPT AFTER THE LUSTS OF DECEIT;
23 AND THAT YOU BE RENEWED IN THE SPIRIT OF YOUR MIND,
24 AND PUT ON THE NEW MAN, WHO IN THE LIKENESS OF GOD HAS BEEN CREATED IN RIGHTEOUSNESS AND HOLINESS OF TRUTH.

When we renew our minds we are defining our reality. To renew your mind means that you are training your mind to be responsive to your spiritual surroundings. Just as we cannot see our natural surroundings without light, we cannot see our spiritual surroundings without light. This light is called revelation!

MATTHEW 6:22-23
22 "THE LAMP OF THE BODY IS THE EYE. IF THEREFORE YOUR EYE IS SOUND, YOUR WHOLE BODY WILL BE FULL OF LIGHT.
23 BUT IF YOUR EYE IS EVIL, YOUR WHOLE BODY WILL BE FULL OF DARKNESS. IF THEREFORE THE LIGHT THAT IS IN YOU IS DARKNESS, HOW GREAT IS THE DARKNESS!

Spiritual discipline requires us to choose what we allow our eyes to see. If you choose to let your bodily senses be filled with darkness, you cannot be a recipient of revelation knowledge and you dull your spiritual sight as a consequence. When your eyes entertain evil, your spiritual eyes become dark but when your eyes entertain good, your spiritual eyes become clearer and your ability to navigate the realm of the spirit becomes clearer. This is what God meant when He told prophets that He had consecrated them.

JEREMIAH 1:5
5 "BEFORE I FORMED YOU IN THE BELLY, I KNEW YOU. BEFORE YOU CAME FORTH OUT OF THE WOMB, I CONSECRATED YOU. I HAVE APPOINTED YOU A PROPHET TO THE NATIONS."

To be consecrated means that you are set apart. It means that you cannot watch what everybody watches and you cannot do what everybody does. This consecration is not just for the prophet, but for the prophetic people of which you are one!

HEBREWS 10:19-20
19 HAVING THEREFORE, BROTHERS, BOLDNESS TO ENTER INTO THE HOLY PLACE BY THE BLOOD OF JESUS,
20 BY THE WAY WHICH HE CONSECRATED FOR US, A NEW AND LIVING WAY, THROUGH THE VEIL, THAT IS TO SAY, HIS FLESH;

We have a new way to the throne, consecrated for us by the shed blood of Christ, but we must take advantage of this new way by watching what we see, hear, smell, taste and touch.

In particular with what we see, we must ask the Holy Spirit to flood our eyes with good things, but we must also be disciplined to set our eyes on good things. Philippians 4 was a good personal rating that Paul would have applied to every movie he went to the cinema to see. It would be the decisive Scripture between him watching Superman or Fifty Shades of Grey.

PHILIPPIANS 4:8
8 FINALLY, BROTHERS, WHATEVER THINGS ARE TRUE, WHATEVER THINGS ARE HONORABLE, WHATEVER THINGS ARE JUST, WHATEVER THINGS ARE PURE, WHATEVER THINGS ARE LOVELY, WHATEVER THINGS ARE OF GOOD REPORT; IF THERE IS ANY VIRTUE, AND IF THERE IS ANY PRAISE, THINK ABOUT THESE THINGS.

4. WALK IN THE SPIRIT

Walking in the Spirit is very misunderstood, yet it is a key to staying sensitive to the Holy Spirit. To walk in the Spirit is not walking in love. You can walk in love and not be walking in the Spirit. Love is not a walk, love is a fruit or product of walking in the Spirit.

GALATIANS 5:16
16 BUT I SAY, WALK BY THE SPIRIT, AND YOU WON'T FULFILL THE LUST OF THE FLESH.

How does one walk in the Spirit? You walk in the Spirit the same way as you walk in the natural, with light! Without light you cannot successfully walk through life. In the same way, without light you cannot successfully navigate your walk in the Spirit. The spirit is a world we are all walking in whether we like it or not, some of us are just walking in it blind!

JOHN 8:12

12 AGAIN, THEREFORE, JESUS SPOKE TO THEM, SAYING, "I AM THE LIGHT OF THE WORLD.HE WHO FOLLOWS ME WILL NOT WALK IN THE DARKNESS, BUT WILL HAVE THE LIGHT OF LIFE."

To walk in the Spirit means you are walking in the light of the spirit world. You can see life from the Spirit just like Adam could in Genesis. When you are walking in the Spirit you know your purpose, you know what to do daily, you live life by destiny and not by pot-luck chance.

JOHN 12:35-36

35 JESUS THEREFORE SAID TO THEM, "YET A LITTLE WHILE THE LIGHT IS WITH YOU. WALK WHILE YOU HAVE THE LIGHT, THAT DARKNESS DOESN'T OVERTAKE YOU. HE WHO WALKS IN THE DARKNESS DOESN'T KNOW WHERE HE IS GOING.

To walk in the Spirit means you are photosensitive to spiritual things. You can make out things that are utter foolishness to those that are walking in the flesh and who treat such things as foolishness. Walking in the Spirit means that your mind is so engaged in meditation on spiritual things that it affects your perception of reality and sensitises you to the point that you can literally see through people.

MATTHEW 9:4

4 JESUS, KNOWING THEIR THOUGHTS, SAID, "WHY DO YOU THINK EVIL IN YOUR HEARTS?

CHAPTER 6 I DISCERNING THE VOICE AND VISION OF GOD

When I was younger, I could know who was walking up and down the stairs just by their foot signature. My mum had small feet, so she would skip elegantly up the stairs. My dad, however, had size 14 feet, so to date, I now his foot signature, it is heavy and slow. I had built such intimacy with my family that their foot signature was distinct to me. We can almost all say that we recognise the signature of our family members going up and down the stairs. Intimacy played a significant part in our discernment. Imagine being so intimate with God that you can recognise his foot signature. That's what the Bible says about Adam.

GENESIS 3:8
8 THEY HEARD THE SOUND OF THE LORD GOD WALKING IN THE GARDEN IN THE COOL OF THE DAY, AND THE MAN AND HIS WIFE HID THEMSELVES FROM THE PRESENCE OF THE LORD GOD AMONG THE TREES OF THE GARDEN.

This chapter seeks to explain what the voice and vision of God sound like so that you and I can become better at discerning Him

TOMI, WHAT DOES GOD VOICE AND VISION SOUND LIKE?

It may bore you to know that God sounds like you talking back to you! The voice of God sounds like the most familiar voice to you in your life. Isn't it interesting that to Samuel, God sounded like Eli. God's voice sounds like your thoughts talking back to you!

Most people I do training with are disappointed by this answer because they are expecting me to point to the most baritone and echoing voice thundering in their eardrum as the signature for the voice of God. I have had the privilege of hearing the audible voice of God four times in my life. That is four times in almost sixteen years of ministry. That means that at least ninety percent of the time I say I hear God, I am referring to my thoughts speaking back to me.

When I see a vision, it is God using my imagination to speak back to me. All visions are day dreams, but not all day dreams are visions. Visions present themselves in the form of God using your imagination to speak back to you.

I will never forget co-conducting a prophetic training with Mum Sharon at a Church of England church. It was the most somber atmosphere you would have every walked into. We were given an exercise to partner with someone we don't know and get a vision of something from their past that they loved doing. Unfortunately to me, the most uninviting looking person in the room didn't have a partner. I ended up being his partner by default. He made it clear to me that he wasn't fully comfortable and so quite nervously I closed my eyes and pleaded with God to give me something or that at least the ground would open up and swallow me whole. I immediately saw a vision. It looked like my imagination running wild! I saw this man on a bicycle in a triathlon, he switched from the bicycle to running, then he switched from running to a motorbike. I sheepishly opened my eyes and he sternly looked down his nose at me.

I said to him, "I saw you in a vision on a bicycle, then running and then you later went and picked up a motorcycle."

He immediately stopped me and asked me who I had spoken to. I said no one! He explained that he used to love bicycle races, but he got injured and switched to running. Due to his severe knee injury he could no longer do what he loved, but that the night before he had gone out to buy a motorcycle. This vision meant nothing to me, but it meant everything to this man.

What did the vision look like? God using my imagination to speak to me. What does His voice sound like? It sounds like your voice speaking back to your mind.

For those of you who are waiting for the Mount Carmel experience to begin your prophetic , let me just assure you with this Scripture.

HEBREWS 12:18-24
18 FOR YOU HAVE NOT COME TO A MOUNTAIN THAT MIGHT BE TOUCHED, AND THAT BURNED WITH FIRE, AND TO BLACKNESS, DARKNESS, STORM,
19 THE SOUND OF A TRUMPET, AND THE VOICE OF WORDS; WHICH THOSE WHO HEARD IT BEGGED THAT NOT ONE MORE WORD SHOULD BE SPOKEN TO THEM,
20 FOR THEY COULD NOT STAND THAT WHICH WAS COMMANDED, "IF EVEN AN ANIMAL TOUCHES THE MOUNTAIN, IT SHALL BE STONED";
21 AND SO FEARFUL WAS THE APPEARANCE, THAT MOSES SAID, "I AM TERRIFIED AND TREMBLING."

22 BUT YOU HAVE COME TO MOUNT ZION, AND TO THE CITY OF THE LIVING GOD, THE HEAVENLY JERUSALEM, AND TO INNUMERABLE MULTITUDES OF ANGELS,
23 TO THE GENERAL ASSEMBLY AND ASSEMBLY OF THE FIRSTBORN WHO ARE ENROLLED IN HEAVEN, TO GOD THE JUDGE OF ALL, TO THE SPIRITS OF JUST MEN MADE PERFECT,
24 TO JESUS, THE MEDIATOR OF A NEW COVENANT, AND TO THE BLOOD OF SPRINKLING THAT SPEAKS BETTER THAN THAT OF ABEL.

Our covenant as prophets and prophetic people is not the same as Moses who had to go up a mountain and hear a thundering and a tangible voice that everyone was afraid of. We have come not to Mount Sinai, but to Mount Zion, a spiritual mountain, which consists of the church, righteous people, Jesus Christ, a multitude of angels. Pretty much a better covenant filled with better promises. The writer of Hebrews then concludes by saying this:

HEBREWS 12:25
25 SEE THAT YOU DON'T REFUSE HIM WHO SPEAKS. FOR IF THEY DIDN'T ESCAPE WHEN THEY REFUSED HIM WHO WARNED ON THE EARTH, HOW MUCH MORE WILL WE NOT ESCAPE WHO TURN AWAY FROM HIM WHO WARNS FROM HEAVEN,

Don't refuse the Holy Spirit's right to speak into His New Covenant assembly! He may not be as loud as He was on Mount Sinai, but what He has to say is just as spectacular. Don't get so caught up in the 'Upper Room experience' that you miss the simplicity of the voice of God.

HOW DO I DIFFERENTIATE GOD'S VOICE AND VISION FROM MY OWN?

God, like us, has an audio signature. When we learn to listen out, we can distinguish it and separate it from our own. The Bible calls it the sound of distinction saying:

1 CORINTHIANS 14:7
7 EVEN THINGS WITHOUT LIFE, GIVING A VOICE, WHETHER PIPE OR HARP, IF THEY DIDN'T GIVE A DISTINCTION IN THE SOUNDS, HOW WOULD IT BE KNOWN WHAT IS PIPED OR HARPED?

God has a distinct sound so that you know it's His voice or vision and this is where we become better at discerning it. Remember what Mum Sharon says, 'God's voice is not heard, it's discerned'.

FIVE WAYS TO DISCERN THE VOICE AND VISION OF GOD

1. God's voice and vision releases heart burn

One day, I was in a meeting praying over a young woman. She must have been eleven years old and we were in Glasgow. Not that I look for a response when I prophesy, but this girl was completely unresponsive and typified most of our children on a Sunday morning.

The whole time I'm prophesying, I keep hearing God say, "Sarah," "Sarah". I ignored it, thinking perhaps it's just me going crazy and I moved on to prophesy over the next person. Whilst I was prophesying over the next person, I continued being distracted with the same name going off in my spirit, "Sarah", "Sarah". It sounded just like my thoughts coming back to me, but this time it left an emotion in me. It felt like fire burning into my brain and setting my whole soul on fire. I felt that if I didn't release this word then I was going to blow up. So I looked back at the girl who is still in the line and I said to her, "I don't know if the name Sarah means anything to you." She broke down on the floor in tears. She shared with me later that, for the longest time, she just wanted to know if God knew her name; she just wanted to know that God knew her. She never had a dad growing up and she wanted to know if Father God knew she existed and just that one word (her name) meant more to her than anything in the world.

What happened? When God speaks and it becomes hard to hold back; it becomes like fire shut up in a bottle.

JEREMIAH 20:9
9 BUT IF I SAY, "I WILL NOT MENTION HIS WORD OR SPEAK ANYMORE IN HIS NAME," HIS WORD IS IN MY HEART LIKE A FIRE, A FIRE SHUT UP IN MY BONES. I AM WEARY OF HOLDING IT IN; INDEED, I CANNOT.

On the road to Emmaus, two men were speaking and Jesus showed up to them but they were kept from discerning it was him. Read how they found out it was Jesus that was speaking with them!

LUKE 24:30-32
30 IT HAPPENED, THAT WHEN HE HAD SAT DOWN AT THE
TABLE WITH THEM, HE TOOK THE BREAD AND GAVE THANKS.
BREAKING IT, HE GAVE TO THEM.
31 THEIR EYES WERE OPENED, AND THEY RECOGNIZED HIM,
AND HE VANISHED OUT OF THEIR SIGHT.
32 THEY SAID ONE TO ANOTHER, "WEREN'T OUR HEARTS
BURNING WITHIN US, WHILE HE SPOKE TO US ALONG THE
WAY, AND WHILE HE OPENED THE SCRIPTURES TO US?"

God's voice and vision will always feel like a burning fire.
Jeremiah said this

JEREMIAH 23:25-29
25 I HAVE HEARD WHAT THE PROPHETS HAVE SAID, WHO
PROPHESY LIES IN MY NAME, SAYING, I HAVE DREAMED, I
HAVE DREAMED.
26 HOW LONG SHALL THIS BE IN THE HEART OF THE
PROPHETS WHO PROPHESY LIES, EVEN THE PROPHETS OF
THE DECEIT OF THEIR OWN HEART?
27 WHO THINK TO CAUSE MY PEOPLE TO FORGET MY NAME
BY THEIR DREAMS WHICH THEY TELL EVERY MAN TO HIS
NEIGHBOR, AS THEIR FATHERS FORGOT MY NAME FOR BAAL.
28 THE PROPHET WHO HAS A DREAM, LET HIM TELL A
DREAM; AND HE WHO HAS MY WORD, LET HIM SPEAK MY
WORD FAITHFULLY. WHAT IS THE STRAW TO THE WHEAT?
SAYS THE LORD.
29 ISN'T MY WORD LIKE FIRE?

2. God's voice and vision hammers on

God's voice hammers on. In essence, God will often repeat
Himself.

PSALM 62:11

11 GOD HAS SPOKEN ONCE; TWICE I HAVE HEARD THIS, THAT POWER BELONGS TO GOD.

Why? Because He wants to make sure that we get the message and usually He is prompting to the imminence of the word coming to pass by repeating it more than once.

GENESIS 41:32

32 NOW AS FOR THE REPEATING OF THE DREAM TO PHARAOH TWICE, IT MEANS THAT THE MATTER IS DETERMINED BY GOD, AND GOD WILL QUICKLY BRING IT ABOUT.

God will often double down on speech and will repeat Himself because He knows our limitations in the flesh to receive spiritual things.

JOB 33:14-18

**14 FOR GOD SPEAKS ONCE, YES TWICE, THOUGH MAN PAYS NO ATTENTION.
15 IN A DREAM, IN A VISION OF THE NIGHT, WHEN DEEP SLEEP FALLS ON MEN, IN SLUMBERING ON THE BED;
16 THEN HE OPENS THE EARS OF MEN, AND SEALS THEIR INSTRUCTION,
17 THAT HE MAY WITHDRAW MAN FROM HIS PURPOSE, AND HIDE PRIDE FROM MAN.
18 HE KEEPS BACK HIS SOUL FROM THE PIT, AND HIS LIFE FROM PERISHING BY THE SWORD.**

Notice, God is speaking here more than once. Here are the reasons He states for why:

- To get our attention
- To open our spiritual ears
- To give us concealed instructions

- To withdraw us from our own purpose
- To keep us from pride
- To save us from death

3. God's voice and vision weighs more than your voice

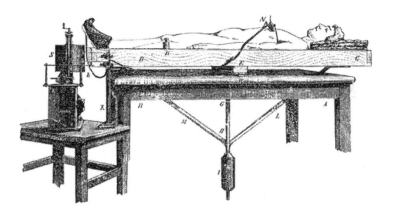

In the late 1880s, an Italian scientist reported that thinking can make the brain grow heavier — if only for a short while. The scientist, Angelo Mosso, placed volunteers on a full-body balance, which looks like a teeter-totter. Then he asked them to concentrate on something. Suddenly their heads grew heavier. On Mosso's balance, a person would lay down longways so that his or her weight was balanced over the fulcrum, and like a playground teeter-totter, the board tilted (lowering somewhat either the head or the feet) as the distribution of weight changed.

Is Angelo's findings a reflection of why the prophets would call God's spoken word a burden. Whether you're a parent or somebody's best friend, we have all discerned when somebody is blatantly lying to us. We know this because when their words hit our ears somehow they just don't feel like they're carrying any weight. Have you ever asked somebody, "What's wrong?" As they respond with the typical statement, "Nothing!" your heart begins to weigh it for density and finding none begins to investigate further. God's voice is exactly the same, it weighs the most on the mind, heart and spirit. This is why Apostle Paul said of prophecy.

1 CORINTHIANS 14:29
29 **TWO OR THREE PROPHETS SHOULD SPEAK, AND THE OTHERS SHOULD WEIGH CAREFULLY WHAT IS SAID.**

Truth has a weight to it and when God speaks to you often people describe it as a burden. It is that which weighs so heavy on your spirit that just like the fire in Jeremiah's bones you feel no relief until you release it. Prophets of old used to call their prophecies 'the burden of the Word of the Lord'

ZECHARIAH 9:1
1 **THE BURDEN OF THE WORD OF THE LORD IN THE LAND OF HADRACH, AND DAMASCUS SHALL BE THE REST THEREOF: WHEN THE EYES OF MAN, AS OF ALL THE TRIBES OF ISRAEL, SHALL BETOWARD THE LORD.**

In Jeremiah, God becomes so tired of people calling His word a burden, that He commands the prophet to tell all the prophets to no longer call His word a burden because He did not want His word to be associated with a wearisome task, but instead the weight of His Word should be carried as a high honour.

JEREMIAH 23:38
38 BUT IF YOU SAY, THE BURDEN OF THE LORD; THEREFORE THUS SAYS THE LORD: BECAUSE YOU SAY THIS WORD, THE BURDEN OF THE LORD, AND I HAVE SENT TO YOU, SAYING, YOU SHALL NOT SAY, THE BURDEN OF THE LORD;

The prophetic, whether in vision or dream is a burden that we have all felt but Jesus says it's a light one and easy to carry. It's a lot easier to carry God's burden than the Devil's. The devil's burden leads to sickness, stress, fatigue and even death. God's burden can liberate people, save entire Nations, change the course kingdoms forever and carrying it is one of great honour.

MATTHEW 11:28-30
**28 "COME TO ME, ALL YOU WHO LABOR AND ARE HEAVILY BURDENED, AND I WILL GIVE YOU REST.
29 TAKE MY YOKE UPON YOU, AND LEARN FROM ME, FOR I AM GENTLE AND LOWLY IN HEART; AND YOU WILL FIND REST FOR YOUR SOULS.
30 FOR MY YOKE IS EASY, AND MY BURDEN IS LIGHT."**

Having said this, not releasing or fulfilling the burden of the Lord can lead to stress, depression, sorrow and grief. What starts off as light and easy can become really heavy and hard really fast when we treat the burden as something we tolerate as in the case of Elijah who said:

1 KINGS 19:4
4 "I HAVE HAD ENOUGH, LORD," HE SAID. "TAKE MY LIFE; I AM NO BETTER THAN MY ANCESTORS."

127

4. God's voice is a whisper

In the Old Testament, God thundered.

JOEL 2:11
**11 THE LORD THUNDERS HIS VOICE BEFORE HIS ARMY; FOR
HIS FORCES ARE VERY GREAT; FOR HE IS STRONG WHO
OBEYS HIS COMMAND; FOR THE DAY OF THE LORD IS GREAT
AND VERY AWESOME, AND WHO CAN ENDURE IT?**

Many people are still waiting to hear this thundering voice of
God. When those in the Old Testament heard this voice they
begged that it should stop. Can you imagine trying to build a
relationship with a God who when He speaks sounds like
thunder all the time.

HEBREWS 12:18-21
**18 FOR YOU HAVE NOT COME TO A MOUNTAIN THAT MIGHT
BE TOUCHED, AND THAT BURNED WITH FIRE, AND TO
BLACKNESS, DARKNESS, STORM,
19 THE SOUND OF A TRUMPET, AND THE VOICE OF WORDS;
WHICH THOSE WHO HEARD IT BEGGED THAT NOT ONE MORE
WORD SHOULD BE SPOKEN TO THEM,
20 FOR THEY COULD NOT STAND THAT WHICH WAS
COMMANDED, "IF EVEN AN ANIMAL TOUCHES THE
MOUNTAIN, IT SHALL BE STONED";
21 AND SO FEARFUL WAS THE APPEARANCE, THAT MOSES
SAID, "I AM TERRIFIED AND TREMBLING."**

In the New Testament, it is no longer God's common form of
communication to thunder. I say no longer common because
God still thunders and each of the four times I heard the voice
of God thunder it shook me to my core. Majority of the times

God speaks to us, it is right into our spirit and it sounds like a still small voice. If we are not careful we will mistake it for our own voice. It is a gentle whisper that is the Lord's common signature.

1 KINGS 19:12
12 AFTER THE EARTHQUAKE CAME A FIRE, BUT THE LORD WAS NOT IN THE FIRE. AND AFTER THE FIRE CAME A GENTLE WHISPER.

That gentle whisper is so easy to ignore. This is why prophets and prophetic people need to be trained in the art of stillness. Waiting on the Lord is the hardest discipline of the prophetic, but to those who master this, have access to the gentle whisper of God. So much as a car horn blowing or a mobile phone vibrating and you can miss it. So you must learn to pray, but after you pray, you must learn to be still.

PSALM 46:10
10 "BE STILL, AND KNOW THAT I AM GOD...

Jesus called it learning how to 'watch and pray.'

MARK 14:38
38 WATCH AND PRAY, THAT YOU MAY NOT ENTER INTO TEMPTATION. THE SPIRIT INDEED IS WILLING, BUT THE FLESH IS WEAK."

We watch to pray and we pray to watch! To develop this balance between watching and praying is key to going from intercession to becoming a prophetic intercessor formally known in Scripture as 'a watchman'.

5 I WAIT FOR THE LORD. MY SOUL WAITS. I HOPE IN HIS WORD.
6 MY SOUL LONGS FOR THE LORD MORE THAN WATCHMEN LONG FOR THE MORNING; MORE THAN WATCHMEN FOR THE MORNING.

Waiting is a practicing part of prayer and every prophetic person must learn to actively pursue revelation through the art of waiting. Waiting is difficult, laborious and quite honestly at times frustrating but as we learn to wait on Him to speak to us in visions and His voice, God begins to pour out His Spirit on us and grant us access to revelation.

God is a deep thinker and a deep speaker and you must learn to search the depth of God in silent prayer and waiting.

PSALM 42:7
7 DEEP CALLS TO DEEP AT THE NOISE OF YOUR WATERFALLS. ALL YOUR WAVES AND YOUR BILLOWS HAVE SWEPT OVER ME.

5. God's voice is majestic and authoritative

God is a king. When God speaks it is majestic and full of Kingdom authority and far more sure than your inner voice. He speaks as one who knows what He is talking about. Boy, oh boy, does God have a sense of humour, but His friendship over us does not forego His Kingship and Majesty. He is our friend, not our familiar.

I will never forget the day I decided to go at 60 miles per hour on a 50mph road. There were speed traps set about a mile apart from each other ready to take pictures of cars that were violating the highway code. I knew what I was doing (or so I told myself) and each time I would come to a speed trap I would slow down to 50mph and once I passed the speed trap, I would speed back up to 60 and sometimes 70mph. I did not account for a speed trap that was hiding behind a tree. When it caught my eye, I slammed on my brakes so hard that the car behind me started hurling abuse at me as he almost rear ended me. I apologised and with heart beating,

I sighed a sigh of relief and that's when I heard the still small majestic voice of God say, *"You know son, only he that speedeth need look out for a speed camera!"*

I laughed, and I laughed! Each time I laughed, I heard Him laugh. It was clearly a jest at my expense, but also a parable for life for all of those who are constantly looking out for the devil in everything and live in constant fear. Just like you never need to look out for a speed trap when you're living in obedience to the highway code, you never need to look out for the law when you're living in the Spirit.

GALATIANS 5:18
18 BUT IF YOU ARE LED BY THE SPIRIT, YOU ARE NOT UNDER THE LAW.

For the first time I understood a Scripture that I had read for years and it turned out to be at a time God was laughing at me for my highway violations. However, listen to how majestically He spoke. What made me laugh the most was when He said '*speedeth!*' I don't believe that was God speaking in 16th Century English, I believe it was God giving me a humorous parable for life. One that still lives with me today. God's voice

131

is both profound and majestic!

PSALM 29:4
4 THE LORD'S VOICE IS POWERFUL. THE LORD'S VOICE IS FULL OF MAJESTY.

CHAPTER 7 | HOW DO I BIRTH THE PROPHETIC IN MY LOCAL CHURCH?

THE PROPHETIC HAS A LOT TO APOLOGISE FOR

I have travelled all over the world from Africa to America and visited most European Countries. I have met prophets in all of the nations I have visited, but for as many prophets as I have met, I have equally met hearts broken, churches devastated, pastors cautious because of the damage that the prophetic had done.

I would love to say it's all in the past but to date, I still find myself apologising for some of my colleagues in the prophetic office or gifting, who married someone to someone they didn't love, or sent someone to a country that they didn't want to go. This is not always evidence of false prophecy, but rather of prophetic immaturity.

The prophetic, although an ancient ministry that far out dates the church is still in its restorative infancy in the 21st Century. It was in the 80's that the prophetic ministry was restored back to the Body of Christ. Therefore, I ask all my readers to give it permission to be born and, as with all babies, to dribble, poo and need to be cleaned up. Please don't throw the baby out with the bath water. Rather, let the prophetic ministry find its feet and become the blessing it was ordained to be from the foundation of the earth.

Some people think the prophetic ministry is a bad idea, especially this New Testament 'all flesh movement' because it erodes protocol to have a movement where everybody can hear God's voice. It causes many denominations to have to question the sustainability of their apostolic models. However, question we must if we are going to ever facilitate the prophetic again in our churches. Every pastor, myself included will face the challenge of a body where everyone can hear God's voice.

Below is a list of some of the challenges and genuine fears your pastor might be going through that makes them shy away from the 'all may prophesy' message.

- Who leads when everyone can hear God?
- Who monitors or validates what the masses are hearing?
- How do we steward people's personal entrustments and build the corporate vision at the same time?
- How do we deal with goofy people to whom the prophetic only enhances their already quirky and unique personalities?
- How do we manage people who claim they hear God, but also have a mental illness?
- What do we do when people start telling us God told them that they should leave our church (and they've only just arrived two weeks ago because "God told them to?")
- How do we continue to have dialogue with people or

journey out when every statement is prefixed, "God said to me?"

- How do we deal with people using the voice of God to manipulate others?
- How do we avoid becoming people's prophetic guru's?
- How am I unique or useful when everyone can hear God's voice?
- How do I protect my church from false prophets and false prophecy?
- How do I correct people who are adamant that God spoke to them?

If you've ever asked or know someone who has ever asked any or all of these questions then let me assure you, you are not alone. Your fear was shared by Joshua in the Bible who, when the seventy elders of Israel started prophesying in Moses' camp, took the sum total of all your fears to say this:

NUMBERS 11:28
28 **"MY LORD MOSES, FORBID THEM!"**

Moses' response did little to allay any of Joshua's fears, but does gives us a window into the New Testament heart and plan of the Holy Spirit:

NUMBERS 11:29
29 **MOSES SAID TO HIM, "ARE YOU JEALOUS FOR MY SAKE? I WISH THAT ALL THE LORD'S PEOPLE WERE PROPHETS, THAT THE LORD WOULD PUT HIS SPIRIT ON THEM!"**

Moses responded, "Are you being jealous on my behalf?" In other words, are you afraid that somehow I will lose what makes me special when God starts making others special round about me? Moses ends by making a shocking statement that unknowingly to him would later become a prophecy cited by Joel and fulfilled in the book of Acts. That God would pour our His Spirit upon 'all flesh'.

Fear is a dangerous thing! It never quite outputs like how it inputs. What I mean by this is, Joshua may have been genuinely afraid, but his fear was being discerned (or at least interpreted) as jealousy by Moses.

Fear tolerated is Christianity contaminated! All the twelve questions listed above are genuine questions but equally genuine 'fear-based' questions. Fear in all things contaminates motive or at least the perceived interpretation of motive. None of these questions should legitimise the abolishment of the prophetic, but rather they should help us make room for the prophetic.

CAN YOU WASH HIM FIRST?

When my wife and I found out we were having our son, people came to me and said,
"Tomi, I bet you're going to cry when he's born?" I genuinely believed them. I mean, I cried when my wife told me that she was pregnant. I cried when we went to hear his heart beating at the ultra sound. I shed a little tear when I found out that we were having boy. When we got to the hospital and my wife was finally in labour and our precious boy came out, I was expecting to be swept away by a tsunami of emotion. Can I be honest with you? In that moment, I found myself trying

desperately to control my gag reflexes. Birthing is messy! When that midwife was handing me my boy, my first thought was, "Can you wash him first!"

Our son, Harvey, is a bundle of joy and a true 'church baby' and socialite. Can I tell you what we bought for this little baby when he was born? We bought baby bottles, rattles, sterilisers, wipes, breast pumps and nappies (or as some would call them 'diapers'). Our most bought thing was nappies because babies do a lot of poos. I mean, we went though bulk sale nappies weekly and it became a hypertension issue when we ran out of them in the house. One day Harvey, like all babies got poo all up his back. My wife and I soon referred to these as the 'poo bombs' or the 'poo-splosions'. The worst was when we were out and you would see it permeate his clothing as he smiled at you with his effervescent and graceful smile you could not help but be in love with this stinky baby.

One day his poo bomb was so bad and all over him that my wife jokingly said, "Just throw him away!"
There was so much poo that we didn't know if we needed to throw away the nappy, the clothes or the whole baby! Forgive me if you are eating whilst I'm sharing this story, but this story so often parallels the prophetic. It can be so messy at times that it can cause anyone of us to think, just throw it away.

The English idiom, 'Don't throw the baby out with the bathwater' springs to mind. The expression here suggests the unavoidable error in which something good is eliminated when trying to get rid of something bad. In other words, avoiding the essential along with the inessential.

Prophecy, like babies, is a beautiful and seemingly innocent thing when it's birthed in any church, region or nation. However, you have to remember to buy lots of nappies because there will be a lot of poo! The Bible puts it like this:

PROVERBS 14:4
4 WHERE NO OXEN ARE, THE CRIB IS CLEAN, BUT MUCH INCREASE IS BY THE STRENGTH OF THE OX.

In other words, the great thing about having no oxen is there is no poo to clean! The downside is that there is also no strength to bring forth the fullness of the harvest. I don't know if this chapter has put to rest any fears, but I sure hope it has equipped you to rise to the maturity of stewarding the birthing of the prophetic within your local church, your region or city. If you remember nothing, then remember to at least buy some nappies and wipes! Birthing is messy. It helps to be prepared!

WISDOM AND REVELATION | THE PERFECT UNION

So many prophetic people spend their entire lives in the realm of revelation that they so often forget that the rest of us haven't yet caught up to where they are in the Spirit. This immature level of the prophetic causes most prophetic people to become frustrated with their pastors or to walk around with what I call the 'rejected prophet syndrome.' In order to partner with your local church to see the prophetic birthed in a nation you and I must keep the main thing the main thing.

138

Revelation is very personal and often we assume that our spiritual leaders ought to know or at least respect our encounters with God. Joseph's brothers got so fed up with Joseph and his prophetic dreams that they sold him into slavery.

GENESIS 37:5
5 **JOSEPH DREAMED A DREAM, AND HE TOLD IT TO HIS BROTHERS, AND THEY HATED HIM ALL THE MORE.**

There are two reasons why the prophetic is rejected by your local church.

- They have built a theology around the fact that the prophetic doesn't exist
- They believe in the prophetic, but are genuinely trying to protect their flock

If it is the former reason, then let me be the first to boldly say that you are probably not in the right church! If it is latter, then I plead with you not to do anything to further enhance or grant credence to their suspicion.

Revelation is a wonderful thing until we share it with people who don't appreciate it. It is immature to assume that your revelation must be accepted because it came from God!

I was in a meeting one day when somebody came to me after and with chest puffed out and hands on belt said, "It must be hard being a prophet considering we prophets get rejected so much by the local church?" My response was, "Actually, I am by and large well received by the local church and I'm very fond of the local church!"

He looked amazed at my statement as if somehow to say that he was more prophetic than me based on the amount of rejection he had received. You are one of two types of prophets in the local church,

- You are anointed
- You are annoying

They both look and feel very similar! The fine line between them is not the revelation, but the delivery man! The question every prophet or prophetic person has got to ask themselves is, 'Am I receivable?'

Somebody once said the prophetic is like being a post man. Your job is to deliver the mail and move on, it's not to make sure they like it. The latter part is true, but I believe referring to the prophetic like the aloof postman does a disservice to those of us who are married to the Word of the Lord that flows through us. True prophetic does not build disassociation between the prophet and his prophecy. True prophetic takes responsibility for every word that comes out of their mouths, asks people to record it for integrities sake and even takes responsibility to pray for the person they are ministering over. Treating the prophetic like a delivery man erodes away at the integrity of the prophetic and raises up elitists whose job is to drop chaos packages and move on, sometimes leaving a trail of devastation behind them.

The prophet must be just as credible as his or her prophecy. Before anyone can receive your prophecy, they must receive you! In other words, you must build credibility within your local church, not assume credibility on the basis that you had a revelation from God. I talk more about this in the chapter 'When is it ever safe to call myself a prophet?'

MATTHEW 10:41
41 HE WHO RECEIVES A PROPHET IN THE NAME OF A PROPHET WILL RECEIVE A PROPHET'S REWARD.

It did not say, "He who receives a prophecy in the name of a prophecy receives a prophet's reward!" I have to receive you first! Meaning that you have got to be credible enough to be received in the local church.

Whether Joseph knew it or not, he was coming across as a threat to his brothers every time he said, "God said to me…" He did not realise that he was terminating any dialogue or relationship with his fellow brothers by prefixing every statement with, "God said to me".

Are you anointed or annoying? Because, like Joseph, you can be both! You can become a mass distributor of revelation to the point that you become redundant and monotonous to any pastor or leader because you did not take the time to marry wisdom! Wisdom will make the one that reveals, the one that is received! This is why Paul prayed earnestly for the church in Ephesus saying:

EPHESIANS 1:17
17 THAT THE GOD OF OUR LORD JESUS CHRIST, THE FATHER OF GLORY, MAY GIVE TO YOU A SPIRIT OF WISDOM AND REVELATION IN THE KNOWLEDGE OF HIM;

You can have knowledge of Him that came through revelation and He could tell you that your local church needs to hear it, but if you do not carefully take the time to pray for wisdom then you will ultimately miscarry revelation before it has even had the chance to bless anybody! Wisdom will make the revealer receivable. So let's talk about some wise things you can do to birth the prophetic within your local church.

1. SEEK GOD, SEARCH GOOGLE

Pray, seek God and find a church or ministry where people are already being developed prophetically. There are lots out there in the digital ether. Make sure that they are credible, do your research.

2. ASK YOUR PASTOR WITH GREAT HUMILITY

Ask your pastor to send you once a week/month (maybe) with some other keen prophetic people to start to learn properly how to administer the prophetic in their local church. Let your pastor know that you are wanting to learn how to be a greater blessing prophetically to your local church. Assure them that you have found a credible prophetic ministry/training course by showing them a collation of your research.

Your Pastor might be cautious about them coming to your church, but they might be a little bit more assured if you go on their behalf and report back to them what you have found out. Suspicion does not mean rejection! Your pastor is likely just being a good shepherd and protecting his/her flock.

Negotiate with what does work. It is not realistic for you to assume that they will be happy for you to take other members with you, neither is it realistic for them to assume that God has not already been developing frustrated prophetic people within their church. Everything is a negotiation and you must build communication with your pastor based on what you can agree upon. If it means that just you go out then so be it, but show your pastor your desire to be accountable by reporting key findings that might be of interest to him such as:

- Does said ministry have a church friendly prophetic curriculum or manual you can give to your pastor?
- Is there any video footage you can share of their teachings or prophetic administrations/activations?
- Are there any testimonials of churches that have been blessed by said prophetic ministry?

3. BUILD A TRUST AND RESPECT DIALOGUE

I have been invited to many churches to run prophetic trainings on the basis of what I call a trust and respect dialogue. The painful fact is that most pastors don't yet fully respect the prophetic gift within their members. Whilst this is not without exception, it is the general rule that a prophet (whether by gift or by office) has no honour in their own house!

MATTHEW 13:57
57 THEY WERE OFFENDED BY HIM. BUT JESUS SAID TO THEM, "A PROPHET IS NOT WITHOUT HONOUR, EXCEPT IN HIS OWN COUNTRY, AND IN HIS OWN HOUSE."

143

Jesus was an offence to his local church and the people who knew Him best. This is the unfortunate mechanism of familiarity and you can either feel rejected by it or learn to leverage it in the pursuit of the ultimate goal. Prophets and prophetic people who allow this to offend them go quickly from rejection to either remission or rebellion. Mature prophets and prophetic people understand that just like baby poo, this is part of the mess involved in the pursuit of restoring the prophetic back into the local church. Your Pastor may or may not respect your gift but they do love you! It is this love that builds or at least can build a trust with you and your pastor that you don't want to ever abuse. Find somebody that they can respect and build a trust/respect bridge between the two, in essence be a Barnabas!

ACTS 9:26-27
26 **WHEN SAUL HAD COME TO JERUSALEM, HE TRIED TO JOIN HIMSELF TO THE DISCIPLES; BUT THEY WERE ALL AFRAID OF HIM, NOT BELIEVING THAT HE WAS A DISCIPLE.** 27 **BUT BARNABAS TOOK HIM, AND BROUGHT HIM TO THE APOSTLES, AND DECLARED TO THEM HOW HE HAD SEEN THE LORD ON THE WAY, AND THAT HE HAD SPOKEN TO HIM, AND HOW AT DAMASCUS HE HAD PREACHED BOLDLY IN THE NAME OF JESUS.**

Joses, fondly named Barnabas (meaning son of encouragement) was pet named so because he leveraged his prophetic capacity to make him a bridge between two streams that otherwise would never have encountered one another. He connected Saul to the rest of the Apostles and is constantly noted in the Book of Acts as being a resource manager (whether human or financial) for the local church. He had the Apostles trust!

An outside prophet will likely be a daunting experience for your local pastor, especially if they call themselves a prophet! All the caution antennas will fully go up but not with somebody your local pastor can trust. You may be that person or you may be the friend of the person your pastor can trust. When you facilitate a meeting, you are bringing somebody your pastor respects but doesn't trust because you are somebody your pastor trusts even if he may or may not fully respect you!

This trust and respect dialogue is what you always want to be a part of facilitating. Your Pastor has one job (many functions but one job):

ACTS 20:28
28 TAKE HEED, THEREFORE, TO YOURSELVES, AND TO ALL THE FLOCK, IN WHICH THE HOLY SPIRIT HAS MADE YOU OVERSEERS, TO SHEPHERD THE ASSEMBLY OF THE LORD AND GOD WHICH HE PURCHASED WITH HIS OWN BLOOD.

This is an incredibly tough balancing act for pastors everywhere and so you must be a trustworthy steward of the prophetic by accommodating your pastors' very serious responsibility and concerns. He or she has literally got blood on his hands if they fail in their duty so allow them to be a little suspicious. Build respect with your pastor by being a mature Christian.

4. BE A CATALYST NOT A CATASTROPHE

I always assume myself a catalyst unless God speaks otherwise. In essence, everywhere I go I ask myself, "If this were the last time I was here, what would I want to leave behind?" In the local church, you can either be a catalyst or a catastrophe. Choose to live like you are here to serve your church, not to help your church be better than it is. Don't serve for your pastor, serve your pastor!

If you have done the other three steps by now you should be negotiating with your pastor four things:

- Prophetic Training - to help people administer the prophetic with order
- Prophetic Teams - these don't replace church leadership, but they do form part of a team that has been entrusted to minister to members both new and current.
- Prophetic Gatherings - special nights for prophetic ministry that run along side the local church and create a wonderfully safe place for prophetic teams to minister to people.
- Prophetic Evangelism - actively prophesying and blessing the lives of the outsider, bringing them to the knowledge of Jesus Christ through words of knowledge and prophetic ministry.

Whatever you do, the prophetic should not be a disruption to the church, but rather should build up the church. The prophetic is not an add-on and the prophetic team is not a specialist unit within the local church. They are another organ of the church just like the worship team, the prayer team and the ushers! They all help enhance the church but the prophetic team helps build the church through building up lives through edification, exhortation and comfort.

4 THE ONE WHO SPEAKS IN A TONGUE BUILDS UP HIMSELF, BUT THE ONE WHO PROPHESIES BUILDS UP THE CHURCH.

Remember, you are not here to set up a separate ministry! You are here to co-labour and serve your pastor with your gift in the building up of the local church! Be a catalyst, not a catastrophe!

5. HONOUR YOUR PASTOR

Finally, honour your pastors. When a Pastor makes room for the gifts of the spirit (especially prophecy) to be a part of his local church, know that that is no small deal. The prophetic always honours and when it does not, it falls terribly short of its true purpose (to show forth the heart and mind of God). I would fail in writing this book if I did not mention that so many prophetic people all over the world have been wounded by their pastors. Sometimes the wound is genuine, yet sometimes it was simply a prophetic person acting out without wisdom.

Everywhere I go I hear of prophetic people being called: Jezebel, Absalom, proud and arrogant and all by pastors who were most likely operating from a place of genuine concern for their members and perceived prophetic people as a threat. Let's face it, some pastors are controlling, some abuse their power but the large majority are simply afraid. When prophetic people don't operate with wisdom, we come across as elitist and it is then far too easy to be perceived as a threat. Honour your pastor means that you genuinely understand their role to the church and that you respectfully work with them through serving them with your gifts, time, resources and abilities. You can't ask for a prophetic school if you don't show up to any of the services. Trust, like respect is built and you and I must do all that we can to be worthy of that trust. I say this knowing full well that there are those prophetic people to whom pastoral abuse has completely eroded their ability to even trust the local church again. There are true prophets and there are false prophets, in the same way there are true pastors and there are false pastors. Don't blame the good ones for the mistakes of the bad ones.

CHAPTER 8 | TEACH ME HOW TO PROPHESY MATURELY

THE FOUR R's OF THE PROPHETIC

The prophetic is made up of four key phases. I call these phases the Four R's of Prophetic Maturity. Understanding not just how God speaks but why God speaks will be crucial to your delivery. My brother, Tobi Arayomi, always says, 'The power of persuasion is in the art of delivery.' Delivery is an art and persuasion is a powerful thing. Our entire jobs in the prophetic are built up of the delicate nature involved in delivery and persuasiveness. Thank God we are not measured by persuasiveness, but we definitely are measured by delivery!

ISAIAH 53:1
1 WHO HAS BELIEVED OUR MESSAGE? TO WHOM HAS THE ARM OF THE LORD BEEN REVEALED?

Prophecy is entirely under the control of the Prophet and nowhere in Scripture does the Lord control somebody to say something. He compels, He weighs heavily upon, He frustrates, but He does not control. To control means that you possess the reins, not just on what you say and do, but how you say and do it! Revelation is controlled by God, but style and delivery is completely within the Prophet's control.

1 CORINTHIANS 14:32
32 THE SPIRITS OF THE PROPHETS ARE SUBJECT TO THE PROPHETS,

So here are the four R's
- Revelation
- Relationship
- Responsibility
- Response

Let's take a deep dive into each one individually and discover how we can perfect our delivery of divine truths.

1. REVELATION

According to the dictionary *revelation* is:

"An enlightening or astonishing disclosure!" In other words, a revelation is God's way of telling you His secrets. When you think of it like this, you will begin to understand that the greatest privilege you can ever have with any being is the secrets that they are willing to divulge to you.

When God tells you a secret, it is safe to assume that He is trying to develop a relationship with you. Sampson's strength was not his hair, it was his secret about his hair. Once you share your secret, you make yourself vulnerable to the one to whom you divulged your secrets. In essence, you give away your strength or at most your position of strength when you share your secrets.

When I tell my wife, "I love you!", I automatically empower her to hurt me. Not that she ever will, but in those few words I have indirectly communicated that she is the only one capable of breaking my heart. A revelation is God's most priced gift to you. It is God sharing a piece of Himself with you and giving you His strength.

DEUTERONOMY 29:29
29 THE SECRET THINGS BELONG TO THE LORD OUR GOD; BUT THE THINGS THAT ARE REVEALED BELONG TO US AND TO OUR CHILDREN FOREVER, THAT WE MAY DO ALL THE WORDS OF THIS LAW.

Some people pray for money, cars, a husband, a wife, children, etc. However, if you can pray to God for anything, I urge you to pray to Him daily for revelation. Why?

JAMES 4:2-3
2 YE LUST, AND HAVE NOT: YE KILL, AND DESIRE TO HAVE, AND CANNOT OBTAIN: YE FIGHT AND WAR, YET YE HAVE NOT, BECAUSE YE ASK NOT.
3 YE ASK, AND RECEIVE NOT, BECAUSE YE ASK AMISS, THAT YE MAY CONSUME IT UPON YOUR LUSTS.

When you do not have revelation, you ask for everything amiss! Revelation uncovers to you what divinely belongs to you and why it divinely belongs to you, so that when you ask God for it you don't ask amiss.

God owns secrets and so praying for revelation is asking God to tell you His secrets. Once the secret is revealed, it no longer belongs only to God, but it belongs to us. What you do with the secrets of God determines your level of maturity or, indeed immaturity.

HOW DO I ACCESS THE SECRETS OF GOD

God will only tell His secrets to two people:

- God tells His secrets to Prophets (the office)
- God tells His secrets to those that fear Him

When God tells His secrets to His Prophets, it is by virtue of their office and the grace of God upon them that He chooses to do so.

AMOS 3:7
7 SURELY THE LORD WILL DO NOTHING, UNLESS HE REVEALS HIS SECRET TO HIS SERVANTS THE PROPHETS.

God takes no action in a nation, city or region without telling His Prophets about it first. This means that Prophets get to break the news before the news media does! God will never forego His own protocol. God is always fulfilling His part! The question is, are His Prophets stationed to receive revelation knowledge from God?

HABAKKUK 2:1
1 I WILL STAND AT MY WATCH, AND SET MYSELF ON THE RAMPARTS, AND WILL LOOK OUT TO SEE WHAT HE WILL SAY TO ME, AND WHAT I WILL ANSWER CONCERNING MY COMPLAINT.

God will always drop the mail into the office of the Prophet, but how you steward your office is the difference between opening the mail and leaving it piling up on your desk. Habakkuk had to be a deliberate receiver of the revelation of God for His Nation. He was a good steward of His office!

152

There are Prophets in the earth today who wait on revelation, instead of actively pursuing revelation.

JEREMIAH 23:21-22
21 I SENT NOT THESE PROPHETS, YET THEY RAN: I DIDN'T SPEAK TO THEM, YET THEY PROPHESIED.
22 BUT IF THEY HAD STOOD IN MY COUNCIL, THEN HAD THEY CAUSED MY PEOPLE TO HEAR MY WORDS, AND HAD TURNED THEM FROM THEIR EVIL WAY, AND FROM THE EVIL OF THEIR DOINGS.

Standing in the council of God takes discipline, it takes patience and time and it is a muscle few prophets learn to perfect. So many Prophets by Office are so used to the prophetic word coming to them by reason of their grace that it is easy for them to succumb to the temptation of doing what my spiritual mum calls 'scooping off the top.' They live their entire prophetic lives waiting for a revelation that they never actively enquire of the Lord to pursue one.

JEREMIAH 23:18
18 FOR WHO HAS STOOD IN THE COUNCIL OF THE LORD, THAT HE SHOULD PERCEIVE AND HEAR HIS WORD? WHO HAS MARKED MY WORD, AND HEARD IT?

God has a council. A heavenly assembly of Prophets and it is in this assembly that Prophets get their assignments. In the morning when I wake up, I deliberately stand in the council of Prophets.

This is why when Prophets share their revelation, it is often similar because of the truth that we are all standing in the same council.

153

God has a council for everything, in His government there is even a council for angels and Satan has a hall pass.

JOB 1:6
6 NOW IT HAPPENED ON THE DAY WHEN GOD'S SONS (THE ANGELS) CAME TO PRESENT THEMSELVES BEFORE THE LORD, THAT SATAN ALSO CAME AMONG THEM.

By virtue of his office as an angel, fallen or not, Satan still has a pass into the council of angels. God still speaks to Satan by virtue of his office much like our Prime Minister or Presidents will speak to tyrants at UN Councils. We do not negotiate oil treaties by virtue of their character, we do so by virtue of their office. This is a vital truth! A Prophet by Office is not exempt from the council of God regardless of how they choose to live their lives. Why? Because God's gifts and callings are irrevocable.

ROMANS 11:29
29 FOR THE GIFTS AND THE CALLING OF GOD ARE IRREVOCABLE.

God speaks to the prophet not by virtue of their character, but out of respect for the Office of the Prophet, God will speak to the prophet. This is why many will say in that day:

MATTHEW 7:22-23
22 MANY WILL TELL ME IN THAT DAY, 'LORD, LORD, DIDN'T WE PROPHESY IN YOUR NAME, IN YOUR NAME CAST OUT DEMONS, AND IN YOUR NAME DO MANY MIGHTY WORKS?' 23 THEN I WILL TELL THEM, 'I NEVER KNEW YOU. DEPART FROM ME, YOU WHO WORK INIQUITY.'

Why will God say, "I never knew you"? These were not false

prophets. These were prophets who God spoke to on account of their office. To whom much is given much more is expected and we must all work out our own salvation with great fear and trembling.

LUKE 12:47-48
47 THAT SERVANT, WHO KNEW HIS LORD'S WILL, AND DIDN'T PREPARE, NOR DO WHAT HE WANTED, WILL BE BEATEN WITH MANY STRIPES,
48 BUT HE WHO DIDN'T KNOW, AND DID THINGS WORTHY OF STRIPES, WILL BE BEATEN WITH FEW STRIPES. TO WHOMEVER MUCH IS GIVEN, OF HIM WILL MUCH BE REQUIRED; AND TO WHOM MUCH WAS ENTRUSTED, OF HIM MORE WILL BE ASKED.

The second reason God reveals secrets to you is because He likes you. He loves everyone, but He certainly doesn't like everyone.

PSALM 25:14
14 THE FRIENDSHIP OF THE LORD IS WITH THOSE WHO FEAR HIM. HE WILL SHOW THEM HIS COVENANT.

Another translation of that verse says, 'The secrets of the Lord are with those that fear Him...' God tells His secrets to His friends. You may not be a Prophet and, like Abraham, you may never give a prophecy, God still treats you like one because you are His friend. The council of the Prophets has top secret security clearance, but the friends of the King have just as much access as His cabinet ministers.

**17 THE LORD SAID, "WILL I HIDE FROM ABRAHAM WHAT I DO,
18 SINCE ABRAHAM HAS SURELY BECOME A GREAT AND
MIGHTY NATION, AND ALL THE NATIONS OF THE EARTH WILL
BE BLESSED IN HIM?
19 FOR I HAVE KNOWN HIM, TO THE END THAT HE MAY
COMMAND HIS CHILDREN AND HIS HOUSEHOLD AFTER HIM,
THAT THEY MAY KEEP THE WAY OF THE LORD, TO DO
RIGHTEOUSNESS AND JUSTICE; TO THE END THAT THE LORD
MAY BRING ON ABRAHAM THAT WHICH HE HAS SPOKEN OF
HIM."**

The Lord was not content to hide from Abraham what He was
going to do. He owed Abraham no obligation to tell him, but
that Abraham was God's friend.

JAMES 2:23
**23 AND THE SCRIPTURE WAS FULFILLED WHICH SAYS,
"ABRAHAM BELIEVED GOD, AND IT WAS ACCOUNTED TO HIM
AS RIGHTEOUSNESS"; AND HE WAS CALLED THE FRIEND OF
GOD.**

Abraham could stand in the council of the Prophets at the
pleasure of the King. He was God's friend and being so
bestowed on him privileges that other Prophets by Office
could not assume. He was able to negotiate with God on
behalf of Sodom. Prophets can't do that, friends can! So
whether, Prophet or friend of God, we can all have access to
the secrets of God!

JOHN 15:15
**15 NO LONGER DO I CALL YOU SERVANTS, FOR THE SERVANT
DOESN'T KNOW WHAT HIS LORD DOES. BUT I HAVE CALLED
YOU FRIENDS, FOR EVERYTHING THAT I HEARD FROM MY
FATHER, I HAVE MADE KNOWN TO YOU.**

THE BENEFITS OF REVELATION

1. REVELATION WILL HONOUR YOU

JOB 29:4-11
**4 AS I WAS IN THE RIPENESS OF MY DAYS, WHEN THE FRIENDSHIP OF GOD WAS IN MY TENT,
5 WHEN THE ALMIGHTY WAS YET WITH ME, AND MY CHILDREN WERE AROUND ME,
6 WHEN MY STEPS WERE WASHED WITH BUTTER, AND THE ROCK POURED OUT STREAMS OF OIL FOR ME,
7 WHEN I WENT FORTH TO THE CITY GATE, WHEN I PREPARED MY SEAT IN THE STREET.
8 THE YOUNG MEN SAW ME AND HID THEMSELVES. THE AGED ROSE UP AND STOOD.
9 THE PRINCES REFRAINED FROM TALKING, AND LAID THEIR HAND ON THEIR MOUTH.
10 THE VOICE OF THE NOBLES WAS HUSHED, AND THEIR TONGUE STUCK TO THE ROOF OF THEIR MOUTH.
11 FOR WHEN THE EAR HEARD ME, THEN IT BLESSED ME; AND WHEN THE EYE SAW ME, IT COMMENDED ME:**

When God gives you His secrets, you look wiser for it and people begin to honour you unusually. Revelation is God shedding His light on something you did not see before and as God sheds His light, you and I become an illuminated being in the sight of others.

EXODUS 34:29-30
29 IT HAPPENED, WHEN MOSES CAME DOWN FROM MOUNT SINAI WITH THE TWO TABLETS OF THE TESTIMONY IN MOSES' HAND, WHEN HE CAME DOWN FROM THE

MOUNTAIN, THAT MOSES DIDN'T KNOW THAT THE SKIN OF HIS FACE SHONE BY REASON OF HIS SPEAKING WITH HIM. 30 WHEN AARON AND ALL THE CHILDREN OF ISRAEL SAW MOSES, BEHOLD, THE SKIN OF HIS FACE SHONE; AND THEY WERE AFRAID TO COME NEAR HIM.

When God gives you revelation, He also makes you radiant. People begin to fear you because you fear God. His glory begins to come upon you and others treat you very differently because of it. When you and I shine with the glory of revelation, it automatically creates honour. Like Job, we begin to experience aged men rising up for us to take a seat on the bus, kings and nobles hushing as we enter a building. Revelation will honour you, whether you like honour or dislike honour.

2. EVERY REVELATION IS FOR YOUR ELEVATION

Indeed, every revelation is intended for your elevation. God will tell you secrets knowing that how you steward it has the capacity to elevate you. The intention of revelation is elevation, although many don't see it as that because revelation in the natural often gets us in trouble. So we have to learn to spot the promotion disguised in commotion.

GENESIS 37:5
5 JOSEPH DREAMED A DREAM, AND HE TOLD IT TO HIS BROTHERS, AND THEY HATED HIM ALL THE MORE.

Joseph's dreams got him sold into slavery. In essence, what got Joseph thrown in a pit and sold to Egypt as a slave was revelation. If Joseph was seeing through the eyes of the flesh, it would have been far too easy for him to be offended at God. In the spirit, God was working out Joseph's promotion through Joseph's commotion. His first dream got him into the governor's house. Joseph then gets thrown into a prison where he learns to steward other people's revelation and interpret other peoples dreams (see Genesis 40). His stewardship of their revelation elevated him to meet the Pharaoh.

GENESIS 41:8-14
8 IT HAPPENED IN THE MORNING THAT HIS SPIRIT WAS TROUBLED, AND HE SENT AND CALLED FOR ALL OF EGYPT'S MAGICIANS AND WISE MEN. PHARAOH TOLD THEM HIS DREAMS, BUT THERE WAS NO ONE WHO COULD INTERPRET THEM TO PHARAOH.
9 THEN THE CHIEF CUPBEARER SPOKE TO PHARAOH, SAYING, "I REMEMBER MY FAULTS TODAY.
10 PHARAOH WAS ANGRY WITH HIS SERVANTS, AND PUT ME IN CUSTODY IN THE HOUSE OF THE CAPTAIN OF THE GUARD, ME AND THE CHIEF BAKER.
11 WE DREAMED A DREAM IN ONE NIGHT, I AND HE. WE DREAMED EACH MAN ACCORDING TO THE INTERPRETATION OF HIS DREAM.
12 THERE WAS WITH US THERE A YOUNG MAN, A HEBREW, SERVANT TO THE CAPTAIN OF THE GUARD, AND WE TOLD HIM, AND HE INTERPRETED TO US OUR DREAMS. TO EACH MAN ACCORDING TO HIS DREAM HE INTERPRETED.
13 IT HAPPENED, AS HE INTERPRETED TO US, SO IT WAS: HE RESTORED ME TO MY OFFICE, AND HE HANGED HIM."
14 THEN PHARAOH SENT AND CALLED JOSEPH, AND THEY BROUGHT HIM HASTILY OUT OF THE DUNGEON. HE SHAVED HIMSELF, CHANGED HIS CLOTHING, AND CAME IN TO PHARAOH.

Do you see how every revelation is an interwoven part of a whole puzzle intended for your elevation. God used Joseph's upset as a set up for his meeting with Pharaoh. The greatest

159

thing God can give you is revelation because it elevates you to greater levels of influence than you could have ever possibly had without it.

GENESIS 50:20
20 **AS FOR YOU, YOU MEANT EVIL AGAINST ME, BUT GOD MEANT IT FOR GOOD, TO BRING TO PASS, AS IT IS THIS DAY, TO SAVE MANY PEOPLE ALIVE.**

3. REVELATION BRINGS YOU BEFORE IMPORTANT PEOPLE

God honours those who actively pursue Him for revelation. There is a famous song that I love by one of my favourite groups, Bethel. It's words are, "You don't give your heart in pieces, you don't hide yourself to tease us!"

Whilst I agree that God does not give us His heart in pieces, He certainly gives us revelation in pieces. The truth is, nobody will ever have the whole picture until we get to Heaven.

1 CORINTHIANS 13:9-10
9 **FOR WE KNOW IN PART, AND WE PROPHESY IN PART;**
10 **BUT WHEN THAT WHICH IS COMPLETE HAS COME, THEN THAT WHICH IS PARTIAL WILL BE DONE AWAY WITH.**

God certainly reveals Himself to us in parts. Any church or minister that claims to have the whole picture and revelation on God is most likely setting themselves up to be a cult leader at least and, at most, a very dangerous individual. God expresses Himself to us in little parts and it is these little parts

160

that hold most prophetic people in deep frustration.

Everybody wants clarity and God is not a giver of clarity, He's a God of parts that lead to clarity as we journey by faith with Him. Revelation is only part of the story of your and others' lives. Every prophecy we give is just a part of a person's life and it is our job to walk by faith in order to see those parts become a whole.

1 CORINTHIANS 13:12
12 FOR NOW WE SEE IN A MIRROR, DIMLY, BUT THEN FACE TO FACE. NOW I KNOW IN PART, BUT THEN I WILL KNOW FULLY, EVEN AS I WAS ALSO FULLY KNOWN.

Remember, the prophetic is a parallel dimension to earth. It is a world through which earth is intended to align. Our job as Prophets is to look into that mirror world and hold it up in people's faces till they align with the predestined plan of God for their lives. The issue is though, because we are human, we can only see dimly in that mirror. However, God will always give us the greatest part of the puzzle. Once we discover this part and search it out, then it is intended for our honour.

PROVERBS 25:2
2 IT IS THE GLORY OF GOD TO CONCEAL A THING, BUT THE GLORY OF KINGS IS TO SEARCH OUT A MATTER.

Does God hide Himself to tease us? I don't know! But hide and seek is definitely by far His favourite game.

ISAIAH 45:15
15 YES, YOU ARE A GOD WHO HIDES HIMSELF, GOD OF ISRAEL, SAVIOUR.

God loves hiding and He loves being sought after. He conceals himself in order that you and I might search for Him. When you find Him, the sign will be revelation. This revelation is a reward you get for searching Him out.

How long do you have to search Him for? I don't know. Some of the greatest revelations the Lord gave me took one hour and yet others took forty days of crying out to Him. For Daniel it took 21 days.

DANIEL 10:1-3
1 IN THE THIRD YEAR OF CYRUS KING OF PERSIA A THING WAS REVEALED TO DANIEL, WHOSE NAME WAS CALLED BELTESHAZZAR; AND THE THING WAS TRUE, EVEN A GREAT WARFARE: AND HE UNDERSTOOD THE THING, AND HAD UNDERSTANDING OF THE VISION.
2 IN THOSE DAYS I, DANIEL, WAS MOURNING THREE WHOLE WEEKS.
3 I ATE NO PLEASANT BREAD, NEITHER CAME FLESH NOR WINE INTO MY MOUTH, NEITHER DID I ANOINT MYSELF AT ALL, UNTIL THREE WHOLE WEEKS WERE FULFILLED.

Revelation takes time and it is those who take the time to pursue revelation that get honoured for it. When God gives you a part of the puzzle, how you steward that part determines what God does next.

4. REVELATION IS FOR BUILDING AND REDEEMING

Every revelation is intended to build something in the earth that would not have existed had the revelation not been given.

God's revelation of heaven rebuilt the earth – see Genesis 1:3
Abraham's revelation to leave his country built the faith – see Genesis 12
Daniel's revelation of the Book of Jeremiah redeems Israel from captivity – see Daniel 9 Peter's revelation of Jesus built the church – see Matthew 16

5. REVELATION GIVES YOU THE OUTCOME

Every revelation should come with the title 'spoiler alert'. God will, through revelation, always show you the end picture. This again causes massive frustration among prophetic people because the situation and the revelation often do not complement nor align.

Revelation is like jumping to the end of a book to see how the story will finish. So when you cry out to God for a revelation of your life, or the life of someone else, most likely that revelation will be a picture of the happy ending, but never the process.

HABAKKUK 2:3
3 FOR THE VISION IS YET FOR THE APPOINTED TIME, AND IT HURRIES TOWARD THE END, AND WON'T PROVE FALSE. THOUGH IT TAKES TIME, WAIT FOR IT; BECAUSE IT WILL SURELY COME. IT WON'T DELAY.

The vision hurries to the end of the story because, whereas our world begins and ends, God's world ends and begins! So we see Jesus slain centuries later, but God sees Jesus slain from the foundation of the earth.

8 AND ALL THAT DWELL UPON THE EARTH SHALL WORSHIP HIM, WHOSE NAMES ARE NOT WRITTEN IN THE BOOK OF LIFE OF THE LAMB SLAIN FROM THE FOUNDATION OF THE WORLD.

Remember, Heaven is a parallel dimension of earth so what we see as a beginning, God sees as an ending. What we see as day, God sees as night. What we see as morning, God sees as evening.

GENESIS 1:5
5 GOD CALLED THE LIGHT "DAY," AND THE DARKNESS HE CALLED "NIGHT." THERE WAS EVENING AND THERE WAS MORNING, ONE DAY.

A mirror is a reflected duplication of an object that appears almost identical to the image it is reflecting, but it is reversed in the direction perpendicular to the mirror's surface. In other words, what you see in a mirror is not the real reflection of you neither is it how others see you, it is a reversed image of you! If you want to know how you really look, take a picture of yourself. This is why most people hate taking pictures of themselves because the image in the camera does not align to the image in the mirror. A mirror will never be a true reflection of who you are! If we see the supernatural in a mirror then we are living in a reversed world and therefore what we call the beginning God calls the end.

ISAIAH 46:9-10
9 REMEMBER THE FORMER THINGS OF OLD: FOR I AM GOD, AND THERE IS NONE ELSE; I AM GOD, AND THERE IS NONE LIKE ME;

10 DECLARING THE END FROM THE BEGINNING, AND FROM ANCIENT TIMES THINGS THAT ARE NOT YET DONE; SAYING, MY COUNSEL SHALL STAND, AND I WILL DO ALL MY PLEASURE;

God lives in the end so He tells us the end and we in our realm look at it perplexed because we are just at the beginning of our journey. However, if we stick with the plan of God then we will certainly achieve that glorious end.

JEREMIAH 29:11
11 FOR I KNOW THE THOUGHTS THAT I THINK TOWARD YOU, SAYS THE LORD, THOUGHTS OF PEACE, AND NOT OF EVIL, TO GIVE YOU AN EXPECTED END

2. RELATIONSHIP

The purpose of revelation is relationship with God. Think of revelation like trust, God is sharing the secrets of His heart with you as a trust to see what you will do with it. Revelation puts you in a position of privilege and advantage against another person because you know how the story ends. The most powerful person in a room is not the person with history but the person with HIS Story! When God writes stories, He begins at the end and when you have the perspective of how the story is going to end, you are the most influential person in the room. You no longer live troubled by what troubles mere man because revelation has ascended you to a place of privilege through which you become a dispenser of peace to those who live in the flesh.

33 I HAVE TOLD YOU THESE THINGS, THAT IN ME YOU MAY HAVE PEACE. IN THE WORLD YOU HAVE OPPRESSION; BUT CHEER UP! I HAVE OVERCOME THE WORLD."

Jesus tells us how the story will end so that we the church can have the greatest advantage against the world. PEACE!! Peace makes us proactive and not reactive, it causes us to see imminent threats to our lives and say boldly,

JOHN 7:6
6 "MY TIME HAS NOT YET COME…"

What a bold and daring statement from a man who lived His entire life from the perspective of the God who wrote it. If we could learn to live our lives in revelation, we will have peace through the process because we know how the story ends.

Revelation is intended to bring you into greater favour with God and greater favour with man. Revelation is an invitation to live earthly life at increasingly higher echelons as each revelation takes you from glory to glory so that you can extend His glory on earth in a greater way.

PROVERBS 18:16
16 A MAN'S GIFT MAKES ROOM FOR HIM, AND BRINGS HIM BEFORE GREAT MEN.

Revelation helps build influential relationships round about you as insights into the secrets of men's hearts automatically upgrades you to places of trust that it takes others years to build.

11 THE KING OF ARAM BECAME VERY UPSET OVER THIS. HE CALLED HIS OFFICERS TOGETHER AND DEMANDED, "WHICH OF YOU IS THE TRAITOR? WHO HAS BEEN INFORMING THE KING OF ISRAEL OF MY PLANS?"
12 "IT'S NOT US, MY LORD THE KING," ONE OF THE OFFICERS REPLIED. "ELISHA, THE PROPHET IN ISRAEL, TELLS THE KING OF ISRAEL EVEN THE WORDS YOU SPEAK IN THE PRIVACY OF YOUR BEDROOM!"

The king of Israel was searching for a double agent in trying to figure out who had been disclosing top secret information to Elisha the Prophet. One of the officers replied that there is a prophet in Israel who knows by revelation what the king of Israel talks about in the privacy of his own bedroom.

I was invited to the United Nations in 2017 to prophesy over national leaders and world influencers. I met a man and a woman who allowed me to minister prophetically over them. The Lord showed me that they were diplomats between two very violently opposing sides and that they could decide whether these two nations go to peace or war. It turned out that they were on the diplomacy team between Donald Trump and Kim Jong Un. We have since become friends, how? Because revelation brings you to a level of relationship with people that would take others years to build. You are assumed trustworthy because you have knowledge of their most intimate bedroom secrets.

I am going to share a true story but names and places will be omitted, kept ambiguous or fictionalised to protect the confidentiality of the characters involved. In October 2018 a dear friend and colleague of mine in the ministry (we'll call her Isabelle) called me. She had a dream and in this dream she saw me on FaceTime telling her that I need to go to a particular place in Africa. I had just come back from a mission there and was not looking to go back so soon, but in the dream I seemed somewhat determined to go. She said, "Tomi, do you know where this place is? It's dangerous there!" I responded, "I need to go there, the Lord has an assignment for me." In the dream, she called the governor's daughter of that state to tell her that Apostle Tomi needs to come visit. The governor's daughter said, "I have been praying for months that God would send Apostle Tomi here". Then she woke up.

Reluctantly, according to Isabelle, she called me, whilst knowing that I had already recently returned from Africa and was likely to turn down a return trip. She shared the dream with me and after hearing where it was, I told her that I would need to pray about it. I got peace from God to go, but I told her that I would go on one condition; that she flies me in and flies me out on the same day. Isabelle was so excited when she got off the phone that she called the governor's daughter in that state and told her that she should prepare a conference for my coming. The governor's daughter just like the dream told Isabelle that she had been praying for God to send me to her state. Everything was aligning to a God who knows the end from the beginning. The conference was set and ready to go when Isabelle called me to say that she was worried because all the flights in and out of that state were closed on that particular date. This meant that, not only would my condition to be flown out on the same day not be met, but there was also no way into the state on that date either. God later on supernaturally touched the heart of a business man to loan us his private jet to fly in and out of there.

168

We flew into Africa and were picked up by police escort and led to the meeting place. When I arrived at the meeting there was a man there who I heard the Lord say to prophesy to. I closed my eyes and began to see a vision. In this vision, I saw this man dressed in royal clothing, I saw his father behind him with a crown getting ready to place it on his head. I saw the ground of this place and this man's feet becoming the same thing. I then saw the crown being slapped off his head.

I proceeded to tell him, "When I stand before you, I feel like I am standing before royalty, I see your feet and the feet of this place as one and the same, I see a crown that was meant to be given to you being taken from you. God told me to come all the way here to give you back your crown. He sent me here from Windsor England just for you..."

The man fell on his face and grabbed my feet in tears of shock. It turned out that he was the prince of this particular city and heir to the throne, but he had lost the throne because his father was a Christian and had given the land to Jesus Christ. When his father died the chiefs, fearing that the son would give the land to Christ, gave the crown to the son's uncle instead.

Since then, myself and this prince have become friends. Why? Revelation will bring you into relationships you never would have had without the revelation.

There is an assumption people have with revelation. I have witnessed this phenomenon many times in my own prophetic ministry. It is the belief that a Prophets know everything about a person's life. The truth is, we only know parts and only the t God gives us.

Jesus met a woman at a well and gave her a word of knowledge.

16 JESUS SAID TO HER, "GO, CALL YOUR HUSBAND, AND COME HERE."
17 THE WOMAN ANSWERED, "I HAVE NO HUSBAND." JESUS SAID TO HER, "YOU SAID WELL, 'I HAVE NO HUSBAND,'
18 FOR YOU HAVE HAD FIVE HUSBANDS; AND HE WHOM YOU NOW HAVE IS NOT YOUR HUSBAND. THIS YOU HAVE SAID TRULY."
19 THE WOMAN SAID TO HIM, "SIR, I PERCEIVE THAT YOU ARE A PROPHET.

Listen however to how she ends her testimony,

JOHN 4:29
29 "COME, SEE A MAN WHO TOLD ME EVERYTHING THAT I DID. CAN THIS BE THE CHRIST?"

Jesus didn't tell her everything she had ever done. He told her one thing she had done. She assumed that somehow Jesus knowing one part of her life meant that Jesus knew every part. As long as Jesus was in the flesh, his prophetic gift was ours, in parts and pieces. This same phenomenon can be seen when, what takes some people years to build, for others takes only a moment because of revelation.

I remember one meeting where I had just finished prophesying. At the end of the meeting, a pastor came to me and started confessing his sins with other women. He said, "You already know this, but I am going to tell you" and, before I could even stop him, he was telling me things I didn't even know and didn't even want to know. Bless his heart, he based it entirely on the assumption that because I know parts of people's lives that are most significant to them that I must know everything. Prophets and prophetic people are not omniscient, however knowing parts does give us such privileged access into people's lives. We must learn to steward these relationships with great honour, privilege and humility.

3. RESPONSIBILITY

Not one revelation comes without responsibility. You and I as a prophetic people have a responsibility not only to actively pursue revelation, but to seek the Lord for what our responsibility is to the Word of the Lord that comes to us. The travesty of the prophetic is that so often that prophetic people are 'waiting for their ministry to begin.' I'd be a millionaire by now if money were the amount of times people came to me saying, 'God called me to the prophetic, but I'm waiting on my ministry!'

Don't wait for responsibility, actively take responsibility. Revelation is the least mature you will ever be as a prophet. When God starts holding you accountable for your neighbourhood, region, city or nation, then you are in the third phase of prophetic maturity – responsibility.

JEREMIAH 1:10
10 BEHOLD, I HAVE THIS DAY SET YOU OVER THE NATIONS AND OVER THE KINGDOMS, TO PLUCK UP AND TO BREAK DOWN AND TO DESTROY AND TO OVERTHROW, TO BUILD AND TO PLANT."

Some put Jeremiah (aka the 'weeping prophet') at around seventeen to twenty years old when he received the call to be a prophet to the nations. God gave him responsibility in a day and before you now it, Jeremiah was the overseer of nations and kingdoms, but he never once had a physical crown. How do you oversee nations without a crown, without a throne and without a palace? God placed international responsibility on Jeremiah and he did not even have so much as a pulpit to launch out from. How did the Lord give him nations and what is the sign that God has called you to nations? It is when He places His words in your mouth.

JEREMIAH 1:9-10
9 THEN YAHWEH PUT FORTH HIS HAND, AND TOUCHED MY MOUTH; AND YAHWEH SAID TO ME, "BEHOLD, I HAVE PUT MY WORDS IN YOUR MOUTH.
10 BEHOLD, I HAVE THIS DAY SET YOU OVER THE NATIONS AND OVER THE KINGDOMS, TO PLUCK UP AND TO BREAK DOWN AND TO DESTROY AND TO OVERTHROW, TO BUILD AND TO PLANT."

What do you do when God has called you to nations? You start in Jerusalem!

ACTS 1:8
8 BUT YOU WILL RECEIVE POWER WHEN THE HOLY SPIRIT HAS COME UPON YOU. YOU WILL BE WITNESSES TO ME IN JERUSALEM, IN ALL JUDEA AND SAMARIA, AND TO THE UTTERMOST PARTS OF THE EARTH."

You and I must learn to take responsibility over what the Lord has given us where the Lord has given us. In essence, prove your ministry where you are and not where you want to be. Every global call started locally before it went abroad.

MATTHEW 9:31

31 BUT THEY WENT OUT AND SPREAD THE NEWS ABOUT HIM THROUGHOUT THAT REGION.

Before Jesus' ministry went national, it started regional. It was carried on the wings of carefully planned and intentional stewardship to one region. Every place Jesus went to was carefully and prayerfully calculated. His goal was the Glory of God and so God increased His fame because He knew that Jesus would use it to glorify God.

The prophetic has a responsibility with it to steward fame with great humility. As God increases your fame you must wish to always point it back to Him.

ACTS 3:12

12 WHEN PETER SAW IT, HE RESPONDED TO THE PEOPLE, "YOU MEN OF ISRAEL, WHY DO YOU MARVEL AT THIS MAN? WHY DO YOU FASTEN YOUR EYES ON US, AS THOUGH BY OUR OWN POWER OR GODLINESS WE HAD MADE HIM WALK?

When it comes to the prophetic, responsibility is the careful and meticulous stewardship of God's dreams and visions from receipt to delivery. In Habakkuk 2, there is a stellar example of an A star Prophet/prophetic person. It highlights not only how to get revelation from God, but how to steward it when it comes.

HABAKKUK 2:1-3

1 I WILL STAND AT MY WATCH, AND SET MYSELF ON THE RAMPARTS, AND WILL LOOK OUT TO SEE WHAT HE WILL SAY TO ME, AND WHAT I WILL ANSWER CONCERNING MY COMPLAINT.

2 THE LORD ANSWERED ME, "WRITE THE REVELATION, AND MAKE IT PLAIN ON TABLETS, THAT HE WHO RUNS MAY READ IT.
3 FOR THE VISION IS YET FOR THE APPOINTED TIME, AND IT HURRIES TOWARD THE END, AND WON'T PROVE FALSE. THOUGH IT TAKES TIME, WAIT FOR IT; BECAUSE IT WILL SURELY COME. IT WON'T DELAY.

There are seven things you must do with every single revelation you receive from God, whether dream or vision.

- Stand
- Station
- See
- Scribe
- Simplify
- Send
- Stay

1. STAND I GIVE GOD ONE HOUR OF YOUR DAY

Habakkuk said, "I will stand at my watch". 'To stand' simply means to be deliberate in your daily pursuit of revelation. Just as there is a place you go to watch television, there must be a place in your house you go to hear and see God's vision. For me, it is my office. Every morning at about 5am, I will go down to my office and stand there for a moment, silently speaking in tongues and expecting God to give me a vision. If God doesn't give me a dream to talk to him about in the morning, I expect that day it's because He wants to give me a vision. Watch towers were secluded places, high up in the air so that people were free of distraction but they also had a vantage point. I'm not asking you to go and build a tower in your house but have a place in your house where you commit to at least one hour a day of silent waiting on the Lord for a vision or to talk to Him about a dream He gave you. If you don't have a dream that night, expect a vision that morning and if you don't have a vision that morning, expect a dream that night.

JOB 33:14-15
14 FOR GOD SPEAKS ONCE, YES TWICE, THOUGH MAN PAYS NO ATTENTION.
15 IN A DREAM, IN A VISION OF THE NIGHT, WHEN DEEP SLEEP FALLS ON MEN, IN SLUMBERING ON THE BED;

Dreams and visions are God's delivery mechanism to communicate to man. Standing means you are taking responsibility to not fall asleep and ultimately miss what God or the enemy is doing.

The reason I say one hour is because it was what Jesus expected of Peter. It is not an exact math but it helps to have a template for prophetic responsibility.

MATTHEW 26:40
40 HE CAME TO THE DISCIPLES, AND FOUND THEM SLEEPING, AND SAID TO PETER, "WHAT, COULDN'T YOU WATCH WITH ME FOR ONE HOUR?

You may be a busy mum, a working dad or a full-time student, but we can all commit at least one hour of our day to standing in God's presence to actively pursue revelation. Sleep is a friend of dreams, but an enemy of vision, so it does take physical stamina to pursue revelation in the day and so standing in the presence of God is the first step to an active daily pursuit of revelation from God.

21 I SENT NOT THESE PROPHETS, YET THEY RAN: I DIDN'T SPEAK TO THEM, YET THEY PROPHESIED.
22 BUT IF THEY HAD STOOD IN MY COUNCIL, THEN HAD THEY CAUSED MY PEOPLE TO HEAR MY WORDS, AND HAD TURNED THEM FROM THEIR EVIL WAY, AND FROM THE EVIL OF THEIR DOINGS.

God is inviting all of us to stand in His council and hear His words but we must keep our eyes open, tired though we may be, but this is our ministry. What we do on the pulpit is the overflow of our daily ministry to the Lord. Standing is where every Prophet and prophetic person begins their prophetic ministry. If you don't have the stamina to stand, to wake up earlier than everybody else and to go to bed later than everybody else, then you will lack the key ingredient to being a prophet – revelation!

PSALM 130:6
6 MY SOUL LONGS FOR THE LORD MORE THAN WATCHMEN LONG FOR THE MORNING; MORE THAN WATCHMEN FOR THE MORNING.

2. STATION I DON'T JUST STAND THERE BUILD A STATION

Build a place in your home that you are committed to spending time listening to God. Habakkuk wasn't looking to be a one off prophet who gave an incredible word that came to pass and has since been his testimony for the last thirty years. He wanted to eat, sleep, prophesy and repeat. This was his daily cycle. Coming to a station point where he could hear God was just as significant to him as a policeman going to a police station. This became Habakkuk's job to the point that he built an entire station to hear the voice of God for Israel. In other words, being stationed means being committed to dialogue with God. You are not just standing there, you are building an integral place where you and God can dialogue about your region, city, nation, etc.

In 2015, I started a programme called 'The Watch'. It was based on a twenty-one day fast that my brother and I were holding for our nation. We had no idea it would become an international movement, gathering nations together to meet us on an online television space to pray for the nation every day at 5am. God poured out words for nations and people's lives that are still speaking in their lives to date. It got to a point where people started to finance us just to hear God for the nations. A ministry got birthed that meant my wife and I could devote our entire year to prayer for nations. We received words from the Lord that quite literally preempted terror attacks by seeing them before they happened. We were right on the pulse of what the Spirit of God was saying for our nation and a television station became a literal station place for hearing God for our nation.

Build the watch towers in your nation. I personally believe that every prophet should be a watchman and every prophetic person should desire to be like Amos, a man who decided to take responsibility for his nation.

14 THEN AMOS ANSWERED AMAZIAH, "I WAS NO PROPHET, NEITHER WAS I A PROPHET'S SON; BUT I WAS A HERDSMAN, AND A FARMER OF SYCAMORE FIGS;
15 AND THE LORD TOOK ME FROM FOLLOWING THE FLOCK, AND THE LORD SAID TO ME, 'GO, PROPHESY TO MY PEOPLE ISRAEL.'

The Prophet Amos took responsibility for his nation. He had a nine to five job and God said, "Go and prophesy!" I believe God is going to raise up watch tower stations in nations that will coalesce with media and become places where words for regions, cities and nations can be heard again.

A station is a meeting place between you and God. It can be a bedroom, a living room, a closet, an office, a toilet on a lunch break. Whatever and wherever it is, you designate it as a space to hear God. Some people may find it funny that I said toilet, but it would shock you to know that some of my most amazing encounters with God happened in my shower. Why? It's the place I sing to God the most. Over time, I have built quite the open heaven in my family loo. Where you meet does not dishonour a God of the New Testament because He has the most honourable meeting place, your body!

21 JESUS SAID TO HER, "WOMAN, BELIEVE ME, THE HOUR COMES, WHEN NEITHER IN THIS MOUNTAIN, NOR IN JERUSALEM, WILL YOU WORSHIP THE FATHER.
22 YOU WORSHIP THAT WHICH YOU DON'T KNOW. WE WORSHIP THAT WHICH WE KNOW; FOR SALVATION IS FROM THE JEWS.
23 BUT THE HOUR COMES, AND NOW IS, WHEN THE TRUE WORSHIPERS WILL WORSHIP THE FATHER IN SPIRIT AND

TRUTH, FOR THE FATHER SEEKS SUCH TO BE HIS WORSHIPERS.
24 GOD IS SPIRIT, AND THOSE WHO WORSHIP HIM MUST WORSHIP IN SPIRIT AND TRUTH."

In the Old Testament, open heaven was very much about location. (See Genesis 28:10), but in the New Testament, open heaven is not about a built temple, but a biological one.

1 CORINTHIANS 6:19
19 OR DON'T YOU KNOW THAT YOUR BODY IS A TEMPLE OF THE HOLY SPIRIT WHICH IS IN YOU, WHICH YOU HAVE FROM GOD? YOU ARE NOT YOUR OWN,

Because your body is God's temple, you become a mobile carrier of the Holy Spirit wherever you are and wherever you go. So a meeting place between you and God is not outside, its inside! However, you must define the meeting place as a time as God will only be as consistent to meeting you as you are to meeting Him.

AMOS 3:3
3 DO TWO WALK TOGETHER, UNLESS THEY HAVE AGREED

The word for agreed here in the Hebrew is yaad it means to make an appointment to gather or assemble. Heaven has many assemblies and whilst we don't know all of them, what is certain is that there are Biblical assembly times that Jesus Himself adhered to for prophets and prophetic people to gather together to commune with the Lord. These are known as watch times.

179

FIRST WATCH - 6:00pm-9:00pm

This is Biblically the first watch of the day.

MATTHEW 14:23
23 AFTER HE HAD SENT THE MULTITUDES AWAY, HE WENT UP INTO THE MOUNTAIN BY HIMSELF TO PRAY. WHEN EVENING HAD COME, HE WAS THERE ALONE.

Jesus began the first watch of the night and it was described as a time of being by Himself to pray. He urgently sent His twelve apostles ahead of Him so He could spend time in quiet meditation and prayer. The first watch is a great time to pour out your heart before the Lord. Remember, these are not just key spiritual military times, but some of your most intimate encounters with the Lord can happen just after a long day of work. I encourage you to build a family that takes individual time out to turn off your phones and pour out your hearts before God.

LAMENTATIONS 2:19
19 ARISE, CRY OUT IN THE NIGHT, AT THE BEGINNING OF THE WATCHES; POUR OUT YOUR HEART LIKE WATER BEFORE THE FACE OF THE LORD: LIFT UP YOUR HANDS TOWARD HIM FOR THE LIFE OF YOUR YOUNG CHILDREN, THAT FAINT FOR HUNGER AT THE HEAD OF EVERY STREET.

Whilst this is not an exact science, and nor am I trying to offer up a methodology, but your first watch should be about intimacy and pouring out your heart like water before God. This is a time to get refreshed and whilst most people try to get it through television or being on their mobile phones, prophetic people can only get refreshed through time spent with God.

19 "SO THAT THERE MAY COME TIMES OF REFRESHING FROM THE PRESENCE OF THE LORD..."

SECOND WATCH - 9:00pm-12:00am

Biblically, this watch is what I like to call 'the turning point watch'. It is that axis upon which a new day is found, so too are the mercies of our God found.

LAMENTATIONS 3:22-23
22 IT IS BECAUSE OF THE LORD'S LOVING KINDNESSES THAT WE ARE NOT CONSUMED, BECAUSE HIS COMPASSION DOESN'T FAIL.
23 THEY ARE NEW EVERY MORNING; GREAT IS YOUR FAITHFULNESS.

This is breakthrough hour and a key time to meet with the Lord concerning breakthrough and that issues of yesterday don't get carried into today. Remember, as prophetic people we are looking at what the Lord has His pulse on and where He is intending to bring a midnight hour breakthrough.

I believe that midnight is a time where the Lord truly fellowships with us. There are no distractions except for your tiredness. This is a great time to get out the pen and paper to scribe the things the Lord is showing you. It seems God takes most of His actions at midnight.

MATTHEW 25:6
6 BUT AT MIDNIGHT THERE WAS A CRY, 'BEHOLD! THE BRIDEGROOM IS COMING! COME OUT TO MEET HIM!'

Paul and Silas were keeping the midnight watch when God decided to do a jail break. As they praised God and sang to

Him during this watch a literal breakthrough happened in the prison they were locked in that affected everyone in the entire prison.

ACTS 16:25-26
25 BUT ABOUT MIDNIGHT PAUL AND SILAS WERE PRAYING AND SINGING HYMNS TO GOD, AND THE PRISONERS WERE LISTENING TO THEM.
26 SUDDENLY THERE WAS A GREAT EARTHQUAKE, SO THAT THE FOUNDATIONS OF THE PRISON WERE SHAKEN; AND IMMEDIATELY ALL THE DOORS WERE OPENED, AND EVERYONE'S BONDS WERE LOOSENED.

This watch is a great time to release breakthrough and songs of praise and worship to the Lord as it is His most decisive hour.

EXODUS 12:29
29 IT HAPPENED AT MIDNIGHT, THAT THE LORD STRUCK ALL THE FIRSTBORN IN THE LAND OF EGYPT, FROM THE FIRSTBORN OF PHARAOH WHO SAT ON HIS THRONE TO THE FIRSTBORN OF THE CAPTIVE WHO WAS IN THE DUNGEON; AND ALL THE FIRSTBORN OF LIVESTOCK.

That same night, as God judged Israel's enemy, He also led Israel out of Egypt. Midnight is a powerful time because darkness and light compete and the dawn serves as a reminder that breakthrough is just around the corner of darkness.

THIRD WATCH - 12:00am-03:00am

PSALM 30:5
5 FOR HIS ANGER IS BUT FOR A MOMENT. HIS FAVOUR IS FOR A LIFETIME. WEEPING MAY STAY FOR THE NIGHT, BUT JOY COMES IN THE MORNING.

A key question to ask God during this watch would be, "God, what breakthrough do you want to bring tomorrow concerning my family, my friends, my region, my country?" Let the Lord speak to you and then partner with Him through deliberate intercession to pray in those things into the earth as the dawn arises.

This is the time Peter denied Christ three times after being found asleep during the second watch (see Matthew 26:34,74). Most people call this the 'witch watch' because it is the time in the earth that most demonic activities are happening in the world.

MATTHEW 24:43
43 BUT KNOW THIS, THAT IF THE MASTER OF THE HOUSE HAD KNOWN IN WHAT WATCH OF THE NIGHT THE THIEF WAS COMING, HE WOULD HAVE WATCHED, AND WOULD NOT HAVE ALLOWED HIS HOUSE TO BE BROKEN INTO.

When God gets decisive, the enemy gets divisive. The enemy is most active under the veil of night when men sleep.

MATTHEW 13:25
25 BUT WHILE PEOPLE SLEPT, HIS ENEMY CAME AND SOWED DARNEL WEEDS ALSO AMONG THE WHEAT, AND WENT AWAY.

It is at this time that the strongest stamina wins the night as

183

you seek the Lord to expose the plans of the enemy. Our jobs during this time is not to see what the enemy is doing, but to intercept him and command that he repays.

EXODUS 22:7
7 ...IF THE THIEF IS CAUGHT, HE SHALL PAY DOUBLE.

It was during one of these watches on the morning of the 19th December 2017 that the Lord showed me a terror plot that He wanted to expose in the Midlands. I began to immediately intercede with our other watchmen from 5am-6am about this on our Facebook live prayer group. That same day a newspaper article came out from the BBC saying that a Midlands terror plot had been thwarted. When we see what the thief is doing, we have the power through intercession to stop him in his tracks and expose his wicked plans.

1 PETER 5:8
8 BE SOBER AND SELF-CONTROLLED. BE WATCHFUL. YOUR ADVERSARY, THE DEVIL, WALKS AROUND LIKE A ROARING LION, SEEKING WHOM HE MAY DEVOUR.

FOURTH WATCH - 03:00am-06:00am

Something supernatural happens when you arrive at all the watches, but it was at the fourth watch that Jesus spotted the enemy trying to drown His disciples. He took action and walked on water to meet them.

MATTHEW 14:23-25
23 AFTER HE HAD SENT THE MULTITUDES AWAY, HE WENT UP INTO THE MOUNTAIN BY HIMSELF TO PRAY. WHEN EVENING HAD COME, HE WAS THERE ALONE.
24 BUT THE BOAT WAS NOW IN THE MIDDLE OF THE SEA, DISTRESSED BY THE WAVES, FOR THE WIND WAS CONTRARY.

25 IN THE FOURTH WATCH OF THE NIGHT, JESUS CAME TO THEM, WALKING ON THE SEA.

I call this encounter time. This is a time where you and the Lord partner together in authority over creation and begin to command your morning.

JOB 38:12-13
12 "HAVE YOU COMMANDED THE MORNING IN YOUR DAYS, AND CAUSED THE DAWN TO KNOW ITS PLACE; 13 THAT IT MIGHT TAKE HOLD OF THE ENDS OF THE EARTH, AND SHAKE THE WICKED OUT OF IT?

Declare to your day to be what the Lord has ordained it to be. Shake all the plans of the enemy out of it through righteous decrees like, "I command you Satan, in the Name of Jesus, to take your hands off of that politician's righteous intentions to fulfil the promises he made to the electorate, in the Name of Jesus!"

Catch the enemy and command the day!

PSALM 118:24
24 THIS IS THE DAY THAT THE LORD HAS MADE. WE WILL REJOICE AND BE GLAD IN IT!

Jesus would often keep all the watches and in no way am I suggesting that you do that. Just keep one and develop people around you who are committed to keeping others that are committed to intelligence sharing. You will be surprised how automatically the Lord begins to awaken you as you become sensitive to His appointed times of prophetic counsel.

39 BUT KNOW THIS, THAT IF THE MASTER OF THE HOUSE HAD KNOWN IN WHAT HOUR THE THIEF WAS COMING, HE WOULD HAVE WATCHED, AND NOT ALLOWED HIS HOUSE TO BE BROKEN INTO.

40 THEREFORE BE READY ALSO, FOR THE SON OF MAN IS COMING IN AN HOUR THAT YOU DON'T EXPECT HIM."

41 PETER SAID TO HIM, "LORD, ARE YOU TELLING THIS PARABLE TO US, OR TO EVERYBODY?"

42 THE LORD SAID, "WHO THEN IS THE FAITHFUL AND WISE STEWARD, WHOM HIS LORD WILL SET OVER HIS HOUSEHOLD, TO GIVE THEM THEIR PORTION OF FOOD AT THE RIGHT TIMES?

43 BLESSED IS THAT SERVANT WHOM HIS LORD WILL FIND DOING SO WHEN HE COMES.

3. SEE I FIVE THINGS TO LOOK OUT FOR WHEN YOU WATCH

Habakkuk was intent on seeing. God typically speaks to us whilst we are awake through visions and whilst we are asleep through dreams. Visions can be visual and audible, or sometimes just one or the other, as too can dreams. In essence, it helps to engage our spiritual senses to what the Lord might be showing us. It also helps to know what to look out for. Here are some things in the Bible that Prophets and prophetic people kept watch over.

1. CITIES

God's eyes are on cities within nations. Why? A city most often represents a nation's financial interests. Take for instance London or Leeds as two major cities within the United Kingdom. If any disaster were to break out in these financial districts it would have catastrophic repercussions for the rest of Britain.

PSALM 127:1
1 UNLESS THE LORD BUILDS THE HOUSE, THEY LABOR IN VAIN WHO BUILD IT. UNLESS THE LORD WATCHES OVER THE CITY, THE WATCHMAN GUARDS IT IN VAIN.

City watchmen are important to stewarding the economic and industrious outcomes of nations. Wherever you are, watch and pray for the protection of your cities as God's eyes are on them and so are the enemy's.

ACTS 9:24
24 THEY WERE WATCHING FOR HIM DAY AND NIGHT AT THE CITY GATE SO THEY COULD MURDER HIM, BUT SAUL WAS TOLD ABOUT THEIR PLOT.

Cities represent massive cultural collateral for the enemy and he keeps a tight lock on what comes in and out of cities because he knows that whatever flows from the cities will affect the nation. This is why I strongly believe God is prophetically and strategically raising up city churches and giving them urban visions.

MATTHEW 5:14
14 YOU ARE THE LIGHT OF THE WORLD. A CITY LOCATED ON A HILL CAN'T BE HIDDEN.

2. PLOTS

Plots are plans of the enemy to bring disaster through:
- Terror attacks
- War Deception Famine Violence
- Humanitarian crisis Virus

The Bible says before every plan of the enemy is laid down, God knows about it and He tells His Prophets about it.

AMOS 3:5-7
5 CAN A BIRD FALL IN A TRAP ON THE EARTH, WHERE NO SNARE IS SET FOR HIM? DOES A SNARE SPRING UP FROM THE GROUND, WHEN THERE IS NOTHING TO CATCH?
6 DOES THE TRUMPET ALARM SOUND IN A CITY, WITHOUT THE PEOPLE BEING AFRAID? DOES EVIL HAPPEN TO A CITY, AND THE LORD HASN'T DONE IT?
7 SURELY THE LORD THE LORD WILL DO NOTHING, UNLESS HE REVEALS HIS SECRET TO HIS SERVANTS THE PROPHETS.

188

God makes no move, and neither does He let the enemy make a move, without revealing the secret to the Prophets. There are no terror attacks that God did not give someone a dream or a vision about, no plague that God did not forewarn a Prophet about in a dream or a vision. The question is, are you making yourself a willing participant in God's dreams and visions?

It helps to know the plots so that you can expose them.

3. POLITICS

It helps to preface this with the fact that God doesn't pick His favourite political party. In fact, the Lord spoke prophetically in a dream to a liberal, narcissistic self-aggrandising world dictator called Nebuchadnezzar.

DANIEL 2:36-38
36 **THIS IS THE DREAM; AND WE WILL TELL ITS INTERPRETATION BEFORE THE KING.**
37 **YOU, O KING, ARE KING OF KINGS, TO WHOM THE GOD OF HEAVEN HAS GIVEN THE KINGDOM, THE POWER, AND THE STRENGTH, AND THE GLORY;**
38 **AND WHEREVER THE CHILDREN OF MEN DWELL, THE ANIMALS OF THE FIELD AND THE BIRDS OF THE SKY HAS HE GIVEN INTO YOUR HAND, AND HAS MADE YOU TO RULE OVER THEM ALL: YOU ARE THE HEAD OF GOLD.**

When it comes to the prophetic ministry and politics, so many people have the proverbial 'horse in the race' that they can't see past their own political leaning to accurately discern what the Lord is saying and doing. Whether we like it or not, political affairs affect us all so it helps to keep a watch on God's plan and the enemy's plan concerning our political landscapes. Particularly for prophetic people from oppressive countries, there is always hope if you are willing to look out for it.

DANIEL 2:19-21
19 THEN WAS THE SECRET REVEALED TO DANIEL IN A VISION OF THE NIGHT. THEN DANIEL BLESSED THE GOD OF HEAVEN. 20 DANIEL ANSWERED, BLESSED BE THE NAME OF GOD FOREVER AND EVER; FOR WISDOM AND MIGHT ARE HIS. 21 HE CHANGES THE TIMES AND THE SEASONS; HE REMOVES KINGS, AND SETS UP KINGS; HE GIVES WISDOM TO THE WISE, AND KNOWLEDGE TO THOSE WHO HAVE UNDERSTANDING;

Here's an important point to note. God will rarely speak to you within an area that you possess little to no understanding, but if He does, it is with the intention that you seek to understand. Let me give you an example. Many years ago, the Lord started to show me dreams concerning who He would elect next in the houses of power. I had no understanding of politics concerning the time the Lord spoke to me and nor did I have desire for politics. However, because of what God was showing me, I began to seek understanding. Starting with Google and Wikipedia, I invested over three years of my life to understanding politics. As I gaining understanding, the Lord increased the supernatural Words of Knowledge to me concerning the future of the nations. Why?

DANIEL 2:21
21 HE GIVES WISDOM TO THE WISE, AND KNOWLEDGE TO THOSE WHO HAVE UNDERSTANDING;

If you possess little understanding of politics and God gives you an insight into politics, it is up to you to gain

190

understanding. As you increase the understanding, God increases the knowledge and indeed the wisdom to be a man or woman of solution. Be interested in what God speaks to you about and He will speak to you more about it.

4, NATIONAL SECURITY THREATS

JEREMIAH 1:14
14 THEN THE LORD SAID TO ME, "OUT OF THE NORTH EVIL WILL BREAK OUT ON ALL THE INHABITANTS OF THE LAND.

God is the NSA director of the universe and He can see foreign and domestic disaster from a mile away. Whether it's man-made or so-called 'mother nature'. Earthquakes, storms, hurricanes, wars, etc. spell disaster for any nation. It helps to know that there is a God who doesn't sleep or slumber and when we stay up with Him, He is invested in revealing to us threats to our nations survival.

AMOS 3:6-7
6 ...DOES EVIL HAPPEN TO A CITY, AND THE LORD HASN'T DONE IT?
7 SURELY THE LORD THE LORD WILL DO NOTHING, UNLESS HE REVEALS HIS SECRET TO HIS SERVANTS THE PROPHETS.

5. ISRAEL
God watches over Israel and they are still His chosen people.

PSALM 121:4
4 BEHOLD, HE WHO WATCHES ISRAEL WILL NEITHER SLUMBER NOR SLEEP.

He still commands us to pray for the peace of Jerusalem (Psalm 122:6). The destiny of the church and Israel is very

191

much intertwined and those that bless Israel with their watch and their tears, God blesses.

6. STRATEGY

If Prophets could spend more time here, kings would have us sit in their palaces, world leaders would gather around us again to hear what the Lord is saying. Strategy is the hallmark of the prophetic ministry. It is not sufficient to know times and seasons for nations if we can't then tell them what they ought to do about it.

1 CHRONICLES 12:32
32 AND OF THE CHILDREN OF ISSACHAR, WHICH WERE MEN THAT HAD UNDERSTANDING OF THE TIMES, TO KNOW WHAT ISRAEL OUGHT TO DO...

When Joseph interpreted Pharaohs dream, it was not enough for Joseph to bring Pharaoh a revelation, he also gave him wisdom on what to do.

GENESIS 41:33-36
33 "NOW THEREFORE LET PHARAOH LOOK FOR A DISCREET AND WISE MAN, AND SET HIM OVER THE LAND OF EGYPT. 34 LET PHARAOH DO THIS, AND LET HIM APPOINT OVERSEERS OVER THE LAND, AND TAKE UP THE FIFTH PART OF THE LAND OF EGYPT'S PRODUCE IN THE SEVEN PLENTEOUS YEARS. 35 LET THEM GATHER ALL THE FOOD OF THESE GOOD YEARS THAT COME, AND LAY UP GRAIN UNDER THE HAND OF PHARAOH FOR FOOD IN THE CITIES, AND LET THEM KEEP IT. 36 THE FOOD WILL BE FOR A STORE TO THE LAND AGAINST THE SEVEN YEARS OF FAMINE, WHICH WILL BE IN THE LAND OF EGYPT; THAT THE LAND NOT PERISH THROUGH THE FAMINE."

Joseph spoke right into the recession that Egypt was going to face, but not only that. He also partnered with wisdom to help Pharaoh strategically get ahead of the impending doom. Prophets must always remain solution orientated because for every flood there is an ark, for every crisis there is a Cross and so God will, ninety-nine per cent of the time, have a redemptive strategy. I say this because there are rare and mitigating circumstances where something is just irredeemable, but it helps to know that God is a redeemer. He is the only one alive to purchase back damaged goods with His own blood.

It helps to know that God has strategies that can help people get clean water, demolish national debt ceilings, cut back deficit spending, boost national economies, prop up the housing markets and the like.

We serve a God that wants souls to be saved, yes. However, He also wants nations to be saved and it is through 'Issachaar prophets' that know what nations ought to do that we will see national solutions leading to national salvations. Strategy will take you from revelation to relevance and God will grow your influence as you become a man and a woman of revelation backed by solutions.

3. RESPONSE

Response is the measure of your prophetic maturity and it determines whether or not God will promote you prophetically or demote you. The number one response to revelation that God often gives the Prophet is to prophesy. Prophecy is the delivery mechanism through which revelation is corresponded to the recipient. It is the ability to be a spokesman for God and a most trusted position of extreme privilege. A position where you can both make or manipulate someone in the same breath is not a position to be taken lightly.

Revelation is like the old Kodak days, long before Instagram and Facebook. A Kodak camera would take pictures and store these pictures as negatives on a film strip. You would take the film strip to your local shop owner who had a dark room. His job was to turn the negatives into positives through developing them.

People often say to me, "I usually get negative words for people and nations, what do I do with them?"

Whether the revelation you get is negative or not, prophecy turns all revelation into clear positives that can be held up to people; and mostly when people see the positives, they are pretty good at spotting the things that shouldn't be in the picture.

I was doing a prophetic workshop in Glasgow, Scotland where I encouraged people, in pairs, to get a vision for their partner and share it with them. I walked past people to hear what they were sharing when I heard a lady in a corner saying to her partner, "God told me to tell you that you're lazy." I quickly interceded and called the woman aside. She looked disappointed with herself and the man she prophesied over looked outright depressed.

I said to her, "Why did you say he was lazy?"

"Because that's what God showed me," she responded. "This is my first time and I knew I would get it wrong!"

"You're not wrong," I whispered silently in her ear. "He is lazy, but that's not what you say to him!" I called her back to the man and asked him if it was okay if I tried to share her revelation again on her behalf, to which he nodded.

"God says, son, I see your effort and I see how when you don't know what to do, you just turn on the TV and disengage with life." (he smirked) "God says I am going to give you an ability to work harder at some areas that I am really calling for your focus on and if you do this for me, I will redeem your time and set right expectations based on right labour and effort."

The woman and I both called the man lazy, the difference was my desire to see him get out of laziness versus her diagnosis of his issue. Prophecy is the delivery mechanism of revelation and so often we as Prophets/prophetic people think that somehow we take away from the message by not delivering it the same way we received it. In doing so, we fail to recognise the intent of God's heart.

EZEKIEL 18:23
23 HAVE I ANY PLEASURE IN THE DEATH OF THE WICKED? SAYS THE LORD THE LORD; AND NOT RATHER THAT HE SHOULD RETURN FROM HIS WAY, AND LIVE?

Prophets are ambassadors and as ambassadors, they stand between a people hostile to God and a God who wants to reach them with His unconditional love. As an ambassador diplomacy is key to seeing these two sides resolve their conflict and broker a new peace treaty. Prophecy is God's diplomacy. It is the power to persuade people through the art of delivery. I am not saying water down your revelation, I'm saying that the ultimate goal of your revelation whether positive or negative is to bring about reconciliation back to God.

Every Prophet/prophetic person has control over how they prophesy and those who claim they don't have not read the Scripture that says:

1 CORINTHIANS 14:32
32 THE SPIRITS OF PROPHETS ARE SUBJECT TO THE CONTROL OF PROPHETS.

To be a prophet means that you have mastered the art of diplomacy and that you are stewarding revelation in a way that influences people and nations to change.

The best example I can give of poor diplomacy was the case of Miriam and Aaron who, both being prophets, decided it was time to prophesy against Moses for the fact that he had married a black woman and not an Israelite woman.

NUMBERS 12:1-2

1 MIRIAM AND AARON SPOKE AGAINST MOSES
BECAUSE OF THE CUSHITE WOMAN WHOM HE HAD
MARRIED; FOR HE HAD MARRIED A CUSHITE
WOMAN.

2 THEY SAID, "HAS THE LORD INDEED SPOKEN ONLY
WITH MOSES? HASN'T HE SPOKEN ALSO WITH US?"
AND THE LORD HEARD IT.

196

These two prophets are manifesting immaturity. Notice when the Lord hears it, what He says in response,

NUMBERS 12:6

6 HE SAID, "HEAR NOW MY WORDS. IF THERE IS A
   PROPHET AMONG YOU, I THE LORD WILL MAKE
   MYSELF KNOWN TO HIM IN A VISION. I WILL
   SPEAK WITH HIM IN A DREAM.

God never once questioned the validity of their prophecy or whether or not He was speaking to them through revelation. He went immediately to style not to substance.

NUMBERS 12:8
8 WITH HIM I WILL SPEAK MOUTH TO MOUTH, EVEN PLAINLY, AND NOT IN RIDDLES; AND HE SHALL SEE THE LORD'S FORM. WHY THEN WERE YOU NOT AFRAID TO SPEAK AGAINST MY SERVANT, AGAINST MOSES?"

He was angry not at what they said but at the irreverent way in which they went about it. To date, I know people who think that to be prophetic you have to 'say it as it is'. This is wrong! To be prophetic you have to say it as God would say it!"

There is a compassion that a lot of Prophets/prophetic people feel is too pastoral to adopt and so, in order to differentiate themselves from pastors, they opt for a stern and mean approach and demeanour. I wish that more Prophets/prophets were pastoral, perhaps the message might be delivered in a manner that can truly change nations.

EPHESIANS 4:15

15 BUT SPEAKING TRUTH IN LOVE, WE MAY GROW UP IN ALL THINGS INTO HIM, WHO IS THE HEAD, CHRIST;

People say, "I've seen what money can do to people". Well, I've seen what knowledge can do to people!

The slogan for my ministry used to be, *'Training people to be prophets and prophets to be people.'* Why? Because something happens to people when God starts giving them prophecy and words of knowledge, they get inflated really fast. I have seen it change people's style irreversibly to the point that it overrides their substance which in most cases is amazing.

1 CORINTHIANS 8:1

1 ...KNOWLEDGE PUFFS UP, BUT LOVE BUILDS UP.

The prophetic is a building ministry and yes, the office may tear down, pull down and even overthrow, but it still has the ultimate focus of building and planting.

JEREMIAH 1:10

10 BEHOLD, I HAVE THIS DAY SET YOU OVER THE NATIONS AND OVER THE KINGDOMS, TO PLUCK UP AND TO BREAK DOWN AND TO DESTROY AND TO OVERTHROW, TO BUILD AND TO PLANT.

Let's look now to a seasoned prophet. Nathan the Prophet was entrusted to go and tell King David that God is getting ready to judge him for his crime.

David had slept with the wife of Uriah, his most trusted servant. When she fell pregnant, he tried to convince Uriah (the husband) to sleep with her in order to cover up his act. When that failed, David placed him on the front line of battle to die a cruel death. He then married the new widow and tried to live happily ever after.

Nathan was given the responsibility of serving King David a very negative word from the Lord. A word that could have cost him his life if the king had so deemed it. David was vested with both judicial and executive privilege, answering to no one other than God. Even here, he seemed to have lost the fear of the Lord that had once made him a righteous ruler.

Nathan had a **revelation**, He had a **relationship** with David that gave him the rapport necessary to speak this word. He had a **responsibility** to resolve a conflict and reconcile David's heart back to God. How he would **respond** would determine his level of prophetic maturity or immaturity. Nathan decided to package the revelation in a story. It is likely that God had not told Nathan of David's sin through a story. However, Nathan decided that the delivery mechanism for the prophecy would be a story.

Why? Because the spirit of the prophet is subject to the one prophesying. You have to train your spirit to be diplomatic and not problematic.

2 SAMUEL 12:1-13
1 THE LORD SENT NATHAN TO DAVID. HE CAME TO HIM, AND SAID TO HIM, "THERE WERE TWO MEN IN ONE CITY; THE ONE RICH, AND THE OTHER POOR.
2 THE RICH MAN HAD VERY MANY FLOCKS AND HERDS,
3 BUT THE POOR MAN HAD NOTHING, EXCEPT ONE LITTLE EWE LAMB, WHICH HE HAD BOUGHT AND RAISED. IT GREW

UP TOGETHER WITH HIM, AND WITH HIS CHILDREN. IT ATE OF HIS OWN FOOD, DRANK OF HIS OWN CUP, AND LAY IN HIS BOSOM, AND WAS TO HIM LIKE A DAUGHTER.

4 A TRAVELER CAME TO THE RICH MAN, AND HE SPARED TO TAKE OF HIS OWN FLOCK AND OF HIS OWN HERD, TO DRESS FOR THE WAYFARING MAN WHO HAD COME TO HIM, BUT TOOK THE POOR MAN'S LAMB, AND DRESSED IT FOR THE MAN WHO HAD COME TO HIM."

5 DAVID'S ANGER WAS GREATLY KINDLED AGAINST THE MAN, AND HE SAID TO NATHAN, "AS THE LORD LIVES, THE MAN WHO HAS DONE THIS IS WORTHY TO DIE!

6 HE SHALL RESTORE THE LAMB FOURFOLD, BECAUSE HE DID THIS THING, AND BECAUSE HE HAD NO PITY!"

7 NATHAN SAID TO DAVID, "YOU ARE THE MAN. THIS IS WHAT THE LORD, THE GOD OF ISRAEL, SAYS: 'I ANOINTED YOU KING OVER ISRAEL, AND I DELIVERED YOU OUT OF THE HAND OF SAUL.

8 I GAVE YOU YOUR MASTER'S HOUSE, AND YOUR MASTER'S WIVES INTO YOUR BOSOM, AND GAVE YOU THE HOUSE OF ISRAEL AND OF JUDAH; AND IF THAT WOULD HAVE BEEN TOO LITTLE, I WOULD HAVE ADDED TO YOU MANY MORE SUCH THINGS.

9 WHY HAVE YOU DESPISED THE WORD OF THE LORD, TO DO THAT WHICH IS EVIL IN HIS SIGHT? YOU HAVE STRUCK URIAH THE HITTITE WITH THE SWORD, AND HAVE TAKEN HIS WIFE TO BE YOUR WIFE, AND HAVE SLAIN HIM WITH THE SWORD OF THE CHILDREN OF AMMON.

10 NOW THEREFORE THE SWORD WILL NEVER DEPART FROM YOUR HOUSE, BECAUSE YOU HAVE DESPISED ME, AND HAVE TAKEN THE WIFE OF URIAH THE HITTITE TO BE YOUR WIFE.'

11 "THIS IS WHAT THE LORD SAYS: 'BEHOLD, I WILL RAISE UP EVIL AGAINST YOU OUT OF YOUR OWN HOUSE; AND I WILL TAKE YOUR WIVES BEFORE YOUR EYES, AND GIVE THEM TO YOUR NEIGHBOR, AND HE WILL LIE WITH YOUR WIVES IN THE SIGHT OF THIS SUN.

12 FOR YOU DID IT SECRETLY, BUT I WILL DO THIS THING BEFORE ALL ISRAEL, AND BEFORE THE SUN.'"

13 DAVID SAID TO NATHAN, "I HAVE SINNED AGAINST THE LORD." NATHAN SAID TO DAVID, "THE LORD ALSO HAS PUT AWAY YOUR SIN. YOU WILL NOT DIE.

What an excellent case study of a prophet who used wisdom as a delivery mechanism for what would have been a very negative prophetic word. He masterfully used a story that he knew David would empathise with in order to shock him out of a subjective justification of his sin into a level of objectivity that turned David's heart back to God.

Had Miriam and Aaron prophesied to David in that hyper reprobate state, they would have likely turned him into a tyrant and filled his heart with more pride. Nathan skilfully and diplomatically brought a king to repentance through the art of right response.

Sharing the revelation the way you received it is like giving an uncooked chicken to your children and complaining that they don't like it. Let people taste and see that your God is good by seasoning your revelation with the love and wisdom of God.

PSALM 34:8
8 OH TASTE AND SEE THAT THE LORD IS GOOD. BLESSED IS THE MAN WHO TAKES REFUGE IN HIM.

CHAPTER 9 | WHEN IS IT EVER SAFE TO CALL MYSELF A PROPHET?

PROPHETS OF PLANES

A Prophet is not a prophet without a mantle. Remember, the gift of prophecy must be stirred up, but the Office of a Prophet is not a gift. It's who you are and so it doesn't need to be energised in quite the same way. Like a mantle, the office envelopes you, it becomes you and not wearing it is like not being yourself. So because of this grace, it is natural for the office to *eat - sleep - prophesy and repeat* because being in the Office of a Prophet means that prophesying is just as natural to you as breathing. Or so it should be!

I remember being on a flight with Mum Sharon on our way to Hungary. I had tried to fall asleep because I don't like heights. I tend to try to fall asleep early so that my brain can bypass the daunting fact that there is a piece of steel projecting us through the air being propelled by two exploding fans.

I had a window seat and Mum Sharon sat in the aisle seat, leaving a middle seat to a young man from Romania. Just as I was starting to doze off, I overheard a familiar voice say, "Excuse me! Do you know anyone who has been stabbed?"

I immediately opened my eyes to see Mum Sharon trying to communicate to the young man sitting between us who did not speak good English. Her communication turned to a game of charades as she began to gesticulate the stabbing process.

I was beading with sweat, not just because she had spoken so bluntly to this poor Romanian kid, but also because she was gesturing the stabbing process on a passenger plane. The young man then lifted up his shirt to reveal a stab wound that he had suffered the night before in a bar fight. It turned out that he was flying home to get away from it all and his friend was still in intensive care at the hospital.

I stood in shock as Mum Sharon motioned for me to place my hand upon his as she rested her hand on his shoulder and commanded his and his friend's healing in Jesus Name onboard a Boeing 747 plane on the way to Hungary. The young man was stunned. He looked as if he had seen one tall black and one very short white angel. He hurried to the back of the plane to tell his friend what had just happened. I sought answers from Mum Sharon.

"How did you do that?" I asked. "Do what?" she responded. "How did you prophesy to that man like that on a plane?" "Oh Tomi," she said, "Never turn it off, remember a prophet is who you are not what you do!"

That word has lived with me ever since and I have learned not to be what Mum Sharon calls 'a conference prophet.'

MANTLED THIS WAY

Prophets by Office are born Prophets, they are not prophets the day they get born again, they are Prophets before they were even born.

JEREMIAH 1:5

5 "BEFORE I FORMED YOU IN THE BELLY, I KNEW YOU. BEFORE YOU CAME FORTH OUT OF THE WOMB, I SANCTIFIED YOU. I HAVE APPOINTED YOU A PROPHET TO THE NATIONS."

Even John the Baptist was anointed from the womb to be a Prophet to the nation of Israel.

LUKE 1:15

15 FOR HE WILL BE GREAT IN THE SIGHT OF THE LORD, AND HE WILL DRINK NO WINE NOR STRONG DRINK. HE WILL BE FILLED WITH THE HOLY SPIRIT, EVEN FROM HIS MOTHER'S WOMB.

A Prophet's calling is inescapable and unavoidable. Trying to avoid the calling to the Prophetic Office is like trying to avoid yourself. It is impossible that when earmarked by God for the Prophetic Office that one can run and hide for very long.

Jeremiah had a rebellious moment where he thought to himself that maybe he could be a regular kid like everyone else. It didn't go too well.

JEREMIAH 20:9

9 IF I SAY, I WILL NOT MAKE MENTION OF HIM, NOR SPEAK ANY MORE IN HIS NAME, THEN THERE IS IN MY HEART AS IT

WERE A BURNING FIRE SHUT UP IN MY BONES, AND I AM WEARY WITH FORBEARING, AND I CAN'T.

It all goes back to the Book of Genesis. When we ask ourselves what did Adam and Eve really lose in the Garden? It is obvious to say that they lost their salvation, their authority and the Garden itself, but when it boils down to it, Adam and Eve lost their clothing.

GENESIS 3:7
7 THE EYES OF BOTH OF THEM WERE OPENED, AND THEY KNEW THAT THEY WERE NAKED. THEY SEWED FIG LEAVES TOGETHER, AND MADE THEMSELVES APRONS.

This nakedness rendered them literally human. It put them in a state of complete humanity, almost as if the clothing was who they were. It seems that from then on, for anybody who was a priest or a prophet, that God was intent on making them some kind of spiritual garment.

EXODUS 28:4
4 THESE ARE THE GARMENTS WHICH THEY SHALL MAKE: A BREASTPLATE, AND AN EPHOD, AND A ROBE, AND A COAT OF CHECKER WORK, A TURBAN, AND A SASH: AND THEY SHALL MAKE HOLY GARMENTS FOR AARON YOUR BROTHER, AND HIS SONS, THAT HE MAY MINISTER TO ME IN THE PRIEST'S OFFICE.

The Lord was very specific in what He wanted those who serve in offices of ministry to wear. Without the mantle or garments they could not serve as priests. Why not? Because just like Adam and Eve, the mantle is the Prophet. When you lose your clothing, like Adam and Eve you lose your office and you literally lose yourself.

When it came time to put Elisha in Elijah's place as a Prophet for Israel, notice what Elijah did.

1 KINGS 19:19
19 SO HE DEPARTED THERE, AND FOUND ELISHA THE SON OF SHAPHAT, WHO WAS PLOWING, WITH TWELVE YOKE OF OXEN BEFORE HIM, AND HE WITH THE TWELFTH: AND ELIJAH PASSED OVER TO HIM, AND CAST HIS MANTLE ON HIM.

What an ordination service! Elijah had just met Elisha and for his introduction to ministry, Elijah threw his mantle on him and then quickly moved on. Imagine, someone you have never met throwing their jacket on you and walking past you. This is exactly what Elijah did to Elisha. He expected Elisha to understand that the moment the clothing came upon him that he and the mantle were to become one and the same thing.

Elisha then pursued Elijah from that day and became his servant. He followed Elijah everywhere to the point that Elijah, after repeated attempts to dissuade him, asked him what he wanted.

Elisha responded, looking at Elijah and exclaimed that one-mantle wasn't enough, he needed a double portion of his spirit.

2 KINGS 2:9
9 "PLEASE LET A DOUBLE PORTION OF YOUR SPIRIT BE ON ME."

Elijah then responded,

10 "YOU HAVE ASKED A HARD THING. IF YOU SEE ME WHEN I AM TAKEN FROM YOU, IT SHALL BE SO FOR YOU; BUT IF NOT, IT SHALL NOT BE SO."

Notice what he said, 'if you see me when I am taken from you, it shall be so for you but if not, it shall not be so!' In other words, Elijah said to Elisha, you are going to have to learn something about the prophetic in a very short space of time. The prophetic is not taught, it is caught and if you catch it, you can have it!

2 KINGS 2:11-14
11 IT HAPPENED, AS THEY STILL WENT ON, AND TALKED, THAT BEHOLD, A CHARIOT OF FIRE AND HORSES OF FIRE SEPARATED THEM; AND ELIJAH WENT UP BY A WHIRLWIND INTO HEAVEN.
12 ELISHA SAW IT, AND HE CRIED, "MY FATHER, MY FATHER, THE CHARIOTS OF ISRAEL AND ITS HORSEMEN!" HE SAW HIM NO MORE: AND HE TOOK HOLD OF HIS OWN CLOTHES, AND TORE THEM IN TWO PIECES.
13 HE TOOK UP ALSO THE MANTLE OF ELIJAH THAT FELL FROM HIM, AND WENT BACK, AND STOOD BY THE BANK OF THE JORDAN.
14 HE TOOK THE MANTLE OF ELIJAH THAT FELL FROM HIM, AND STRUCK THE WATERS, AND SAID, "WHERE IS THE LORD, THE GOD OF ELIJAH?" WHEN HE ALSO HAD STRUCK THE WATERS, THEY WERE DIVIDED HERE AND THERE; AND ELISHA WENT OVER.

Elisha understood the mystery. Elijah wasn't the body that went up, Elisha was the mantle that came down. The reason many people miss their ministry is because they follow a man and not a mantle. Elisha understood from that moment, the mantle was Elijah, not the flesh that ascended that day. He picked up the spirit of Elijah when he took up the mantle. He learnt in a day what experienced prophets around him still did not understand.

15 WHEN THE SONS OF THE PROPHETS WHO WERE AT JERICHO OVER AGAINST HIM SAW HIM, THEY SAID, "THE SPIRIT OF ELIJAH RESTS ON ELISHA." THEY CAME TO MEET HIM, AND BOWED THEMSELVES TO THE GROUND BEFORE HIM.
16 THEY SAID TO HIM, "SEE NOW, THERE ARE WITH YOUR SERVANTS FIFTY STRONG MEN. PLEASE LET THEM GO AND SEEK YOUR MASTER. PERHAPS THE SPIRIT OF THE LORD HAS TAKEN HIM UP, AND PUT HIM ON SOME MOUNTAIN, OR INTO SOME VALLEY. HE SAID, "YOU SHALL NOT SEND THEM."
17 WHEN THEY URGED HIM UNTIL HE WAS ASHAMED, HE SAID, "SEND THEM." THEY SENT THEREFORE FIFTY MEN; AND THEY SEARCHED FOR THREE DAYS, BUT DIDN'T FIND HIM.

They were looking for a man, whilst Elisha was looking for a mantle and so his ministry got birthed that day because he caught what they were only content with being taught.

Jesus tried to teach this to his disciples but they still didn't get it.

LUKE 8:43-44
43 A WOMAN WHO HAD A FLOW OF BLOOD FOR TWELVE YEARS, WHO HAD SPENT ALL HER LIVING ON PHYSICIANS, AND COULD NOT BE HEALED BY ANY,
44 CAME BEHIND HIM, AND TOUCHED THE FRINGE OF HIS CLOAK, AND IMMEDIATELY THE FLOW OF HER BLOOD STOPPED.

This woman who had an issue of blood understood that, just

as Adam was the spirit that clothed him and Elijah was the spirit that clothed him, Jesus was not the man but the mantle that clothed him. She reached out and touched him before running away. Listen to what Jesus then said.

LUKE 8:45
45 JESUS SAID, "WHO TOUCHED ME?" WHEN ALL DENIED IT, PETER AND THOSE WITH HIM SAID, "MASTER, THE MULTITUDES PRESS AND JOSTLE YOU, AND YOU SAY, 'WHO TOUCHED ME?'"

How is it remotely possible that a man can feel His clothes being touched. Apostle Peter looked at Jesus perplexed saying,

LUKE 8:45
45...MASTER, THE MULTITUDES PRESS AND JOSTLE YOU, AND YOU SAY, 'WHO TOUCHED ME?'"

The multitudes touched Jesus body, but the woman touched Jesus right at the core of his office. She understood that this is not taught it is caught.

> LUKE 8:46
> **46 BUT JESUS SAID, "SOMEONE DID TOUCH ME, FOR I PERCEIVED THAT POWER HAS GONE OUT OF ME."**

Notice Jesus did not say, someone touched my garments. He said, "Someone touched Me!" The mantle is who you are! You don't ever to take it off. The day you do, you're as good as dead.

209

28 MOSES STRIPPED AARON OF HIS GARMENTS, AND PUT THEM ON ELEAZAR HIS SON; AND AARON DIED THERE ON THE TOP OF THE MOUNTAIN

PROVE YOUR MINISTRY

In my experience, it's never safe to call yourself a Prophet. It is far safer for others to call you one than for you to commend yourself. The worst thing you can do as a Prophet is act entitled. I once knew a pastor's kid who, when she was younger, used to storm into her dad's office when he was in important meetings and just hug him and boss everyone around. As she grew older, she tried to carry on much in the same way, but her dad was no longer having it. He told her, "From now on, when you come in here, you knock like everyone else. If you want a job here, you're going to have to apply like everyone else."

She had assumed that because she was the daughter of the pastor that she had special privileges to boss around all of his co-workers. She had grown entitled and that's the case of many who believe they are called to the prophetic.

Can you imagine when Satan came to challenge Jesus' sonship in Matthew 4, Jesus saying, "Of course I am the Son of God, didn't you hear what He said about me when the heavens opened"?

No, instead Jesus simply responded, "It is written..." Jesus was not willing to fight the enemy out of entitlement. In fact, Jesus' ministry was proven on four levels:

1. God

MATTHEW 3:17
17 BEHOLD, A VOICE OUT OF THE HEAVENS SAID, "THIS IS MY BELOVED SON, WITH WHOM I AM WELL PLEASED."

2. The Devil and Demons

LUKE 4:41
41 DEMONS ALSO CAME OUT FROM MANY, CRYING OUT, AND SAYING, "YOU ARE THE CHRIST, THE SON OF GOD!" REBUKING THEM, HE DIDN'T ALLOW THEM TO SPEAK, BECAUSE THEY KNEW THAT HE WAS THE CHRIST.

3. Man

MATTHEW 16:15-16
15 HE SAID TO THEM, "BUT WHO DO YOU SAY THAT I AM?"
16 SIMON PETER ANSWERED, "YOU ARE THE CHRIST, THE SON OF THE LIVING GOD."

4. Creation

LUKE 9:34-35
34 WHILE HE SAID THESE THINGS, A CLOUD CAME AND OVERSHADOWED THEM, AND THEY WERE AFRAID AS THEY ENTERED INTO THE CLOUD.
35 A VOICE CAME OUT OF THE CLOUD, SAYING, "THIS IS MY BELOVED SON. LISTEN TO HIM!

Whether you know it or not, we are all called to prove our ministry on these four levels.

2 TIMOTHY 4:5

5 BUT YOU BE SOBER IN ALL THINGS, SUFFER HARDSHIP, DO THE WORK OF AN EVANGELIST, AND PROVE YOUR MINISTRY.

Just because God has approved you doesn't mean that man, Satan or creation will do the same . Many spiritual leaders are content with the approval of men and whilst this is important to the growth of your ministry, when approval with man is the ultimate goal, you will ultimately sacrifice God's approval to get it.

The biggest question on most Prophets' hearts is, "When does my ministry start?" Most people who ask this feel disgruntled at the delay in the lack of opportunity. What they are often waiting for is a pulpit and a man to approve them so that they can be everything God has ordained them to be. In doing so, they fail to realise that when God approves you, then your light will speak for you and it becomes impossible for man to not see you.

MATTHEW 5:14

14 YOU ARE THE LIGHT OF THE WORLD. A CITY LOCATED ON A HILL CAN'T BE HIDDEN.

When you shine with your office, then the church and the world, whether for good or for bad, will pay attention. Light doesn't talk, it shines. For men to call you a pastor, you should at least have a Congregation. For men to call you an evangelist, you should at least win a soul. For men to call you an apostle, you should at least carry revelation and plant a church and pioneer in the new. For men to call you a prophet, the least you can do is prophesy!

I have seen many prophets who don't prophesy. Of the ones that do prophesy, I have witnessed that they have not taken the time to truly catch the prophetic to the extent that they know how to be a diplomat in the deliberation of how they steward their calling. These prophets assume acceptance and then get rejection because they do not realise that, just because God calls you prophet, doesn't mean that man does! You and I must prove our ministry on every level.

HOW TO STEWARD YOUR PROPHETIC CALLING TO A PLACE OF RECOGNITION

1. BE CHRIST MINDED

In order for Jesus to change the world, it was not enough for the heavens to open and for God to say, "This is My Son in whom I am well pleased!" He could not take that argument to mankind and try to convince them that based on his revelation that people should receive him. He needed the wisdom of God.

LUKE 2:52
52 **AND JESUS INCREASED IN WISDOM AND STATURE, AND IN FAVOUR WITH GOD AND MEN.**

Wisdom brought Jesus into favour with man; favour He had to learn to increase in. Jesus did not assume anything! If anyone should have had a spirit of entitlement it should have been the one to whom nothing needs to be revealed because He knew all things in Heaven. He still had to be likeable. People still chose and still choose to this day whether to like or not to like Him or receive Him.

JOHN 1:10-12
**10 HE WAS IN THE WORLD, AND THE WORLD WAS MADE THROUGH HIM, AND THE WORLD DIDN'T RECOGNISE HIM.
11 HE CAME TO HIS OWN, AND THOSE WHO WERE HIS OWN DIDN'T RECEIVE HIM.
12 BUT AS MANY AS RECEIVED HIM, TO THEM HE GAVE THE RIGHT TO BECOME GOD'S CHILDREN, TO THOSE WHO BELIEVE IN HIS NAME:**

Jesus didn't live his whole life feeling rejected about people not receiving or recognising Him. The fact that people don't receive Him today doesn't make Him any less God or in any way insecure.

Jesus didn't carry a spirit of entitlement. Jesus knew that He was going to do His best to make Himself as receivable as possible by behaving wisely around people. He packaged His gift in the love and wisdom of God so that there was no excuse not to receive Him.

However, many prophets today believe that people don't need to like them. This is the danger of the 'delivery man' mentality! It people thinking that the meaner and the less pastoral that they are, that the more prophetic they are. This is simply not true! Revelation does not entitle the revealer any more than sonship with God entitled Christ!

PHILIPPIANS 2:5-11
5 LET THIS MIND BE IN YOU, WHICH WAS ALSO IN CHRIST JESUS,

6 WHO, EXISTING IN THE FORM OF GOD, DIDN'T CONSIDER EQUALITY WITH GOD A THING TO BE GRASPED,
7 BUT EMPTIED HIMSELF, TAKING THE FORM OF A SERVANT, BEING MADE IN THE LIKENESS OF MEN.
8 AND BEING FOUND IN HUMAN FORM, HE HUMBLED HIMSELF, BECOMING OBEDIENT TO DEATH, YES, THE DEATH OF THE CROSS.
9 THEREFORE GOD ALSO HIGHLY EXALTED HIM, AND GAVE TO HIM THE NAME WHICH IS ABOVE EVERY NAME;
10 THAT AT THE NAME OF JESUS EVERY KNEE SHOULD BOW, OF THOSE IN HEAVEN, THOSE ON EARTH, AND THOSE UNDER THE EARTH,
11 AND THAT EVERY TONGUE SHOULD CONFESS THAT JESUS CHRIST IS LORD, TO THE GLORY OF GOD THE FATHER.

2. BE LIKEABLE

Sometimes you will see these little tests you can do online to determine if you are a prophet. It will normally lists a bunch of questions like:

- Do you dream and have visions.
- Are you impatient with others
- Do you find yourself leading others more than being led

The list will go on until you realise that somehow because you are impatient with others you are a prophet. The only Biblical litmus test for the prophetic is 'that what you say comes to pass' (Deuteronomy 18:21-22)

Mean people aren't prophets, they're just mean and intolerant people. That's not a gift issue, that's a fruit and character issue. The prophetic is not a popularity contest, but you do have to be likeable!

215

PROVERBS 18:24
24 **A MAN WITH FRIENDS IS TO SHOW HIMSELF FRIENDLY, AND THERE IS A LOVER ADHERING MORE THAN A BROTHER!**

If you want friends, be friendly!

You don't need many friends, but you certainly need the right ones if you are going to birth the prophetic. Remember, carrying a spirit of entitlement is costly to the prophetic assignment. I don't mean you should be friendly for the sake of birthing the prophetic in the nation. I mean be friendly because it is a part of the nature of Christ. Some people think that their gift or office should make them miserable. I always like to point them to Galatians 5:22 which talks about the fruit of the Spirit. In other words, you must cultivate in your daily walk fruit so that when churches, regions and nations taste of it, they receive your gift.

EZEKIEL 47:12
12 **BY THE RIVER ON ITS BANK, ON THIS SIDE AND ON THAT SIDE, SHALL GROW EVERY TREE FOR FOOD, WHOSE LEAF SHALL NOT WITHER, NEITHER SHALL ITS FRUIT FAIL: IT SHALL BRING FORTH NEW FRUIT EVERY MONTH, BECAUSE ITS WATERS ISSUE OUT OF THE SANCTUARY; AND ITS FRUIT SHALL BE FOR FOOD, AND ITS LEAF FOR HEALING.**

God says, He is going to make you a tree and that your church will taste the fruit and want the gift. The maturity of any tree is not the leaves, but the fruit! You can possess the greatest gifts of healing, prophecy and tongues, but if your fruit is bitter then even if your leaves are wonderful you will not be received.

15 "BEWARE OF FALSE PROPHETS, WHO COME TO YOU IN SHEEP'S CLOTHING, BUT INWARDLY ARE RAVENING WOLVES. 16 BY THEIR FRUITS YOU WILL KNOW THEM. DO YOU GATHER GRAPES FROM THORNS, OR FIGS FROM THISTLES?

False prophets don't all have false leaves, they just have false fruits! In other words, although a false prophet can have a true word, a false heart will manipulate a true word. Jesus did not say that you shall know them by their leaves, but by the fruit of their lives! This brings me to a most salient point.

3. BE CREDIBLE

Be accountable to someone whose prophetic call is greater than your own. I can't tell you how much my proximity to Mum Sharon has bolstered my credibility as a Prophet. Gleaning from her has refined my character and reproduced in me right motive for the prophetic and her reputation has also endorsed mine.

Even Jesus needed a character witness to go ahead of Him.

JOHN 1:6-9
6 THERE CAME A MAN, SENT FROM GOD, WHOSE NAME WAS JOHN.
7 THE SAME CAME AS A WITNESS, THAT HE MIGHT TESTIFY ABOUT THE LIGHT, THAT ALL MIGHT BELIEVE THROUGH HIM.
8 HE WAS NOT THE LIGHT, BUT WAS SENT THAT HE MIGHT TESTIFY ABOUT THE LIGHT.
9 THE TRUE LIGHT THAT ENLIGHTENS EVERYONE WAS COMING INTO THE WORLD.

John lived his entire life endorsing the ministry of Jesus and by this time his ministry was already credible. He was a character witness for the one being with the most astute character in the universe.

JOHN 1:15
15 JOHN TESTIFIED ABOUT HIM. HE CRIED OUT, SAYING, "THIS WAS HE OF WHOM I SAID, 'HE WHO COMES AFTER ME HAS SURPASSED ME, FOR HE WAS BEFORE ME.'"

Prophets without credible spiritual fathers and mothers in the prophetic are perceived as a threat to everyone. Credible means that someone with weight and influence can speak for you that you are submitted, honourable, servant hearted and that you are not connected to said ministry just so you can use them to get acclaim for yourself.

I met a woman who asked me to be her mentor and spiritual covering. I agreed, but reluctantly because she lived too far away from me and I'm a firm believer in proximity discipleship. When Jesus said "Follow me", He didn't mean on Twitter! He meant leave what you are doing and join your life to mine to acquire what I have. It wasn't long before I realised that I had more work than months and my ability to commit to once a week 'FaceTime' calls was becoming more and more unrealistic. I remember calling her one day from an airport to apologise for not being in touch.

She responded, "That's okay, God spoke to me and said I don't need a spiritual mentor, that because of my prophetic office, that He was going to teach me and cover me!"

I felt great disappointment in her response, but I also felt the opinion of so many I have come into contact with on the prophetic journey. There is a certain pride that often follows the prophetic and makes it so easy for the enemy to hijack communication. When you are no longer accountable, you are no longer credible. You have automatically set yourself up for rejection in a ministry that is already prone to rejecting people when you refuse to be accountable. Isolated prophets are dangerous because they don't know how easy it is for a spirit of error and deception to intercept their communication.

PROVERBS 18:1
1 WHOEVER ISOLATES HIMSELF SEEKS HIS OWN DESIRE; HE BREAKS OUT AGAINST ALL SOUND JUDGMENT.

Jesus never spoke on His own account, the fruit spoke for itself.

JOHN 5:31-32
31 "IF I TESTIFY ABOUT MYSELF, MY WITNESS IS NOT VALID.

32 IT IS ANOTHER WHO TESTIFIES ABOUT ME. I KNOW THAT THE TESTIMONY WHICH HE TESTIFIES ABOUT ME IS TRUE.

Whilst character is what others say about you, credibility is what others say about your results! Ultimately, credibility is not the ability to be likeable, it is the ability to reproduce results.

JOHN 5:36
36 BUT THE TESTIMONY WHICH I HAVE IS GREATER THAN THAT OF JOHN, FOR THE WORKS WHICH THE FATHER GAVE ME TO ACCOMPLISH, THE VERY WORKS THAT I DO, TESTIFY ABOUT ME, THAT THE FATHER HAS SENT ME.

Eventually, an endorsement is not enough. Your works must endorse you. An endorsement is a platform to give you access, but if you don't let your fruit speak for you then not even an endorsement can help you.

If your desire to be incredible trumps your desire to be credible, then you will damage your credibility in the process! Your authority doesn't grow with how nice you are, your authority grows based on your track record. Track record is not what you say about yourself, it is what others say about you!

4. SHINE

MATTHEW 5:16
16 EVEN SO, LET YOUR LIGHT SHINE BEFORE MEN; THAT THEY MAY SEE YOUR GOOD WORKS, AND GLORIFY YOUR FATHER WHO IS IN HEAVEN.

This is not about letting your show shine, but about letting your shine show!

Shining means that your gift speaks for you without need for extra bells, whistles or quirky personalities. Speaking into people's lives or nations is a privilege, not a right, and people only truly receive your gift based on its track record.

MARK 5:27
27 SHE HAD HEARD THE REPORTS ABOUT JESUS AND CAME UP BEHIND HIM IN THE CROWD AND TOUCHED HIS GARMENT.

You shine as a prophet when you are prophesying or prophetically preaching. Don't be afraid to shine.

5. LEAN TOWARDS THE WORD OF KNOWLEDGE

The word of knowledge is a fast track to national prophetic recognition. Prophets who lean on a word of prophecy have to wait for the word to have its fulfilment before they are endorsed as a prophet.

EZEKIEL 33:32-33
33 BEHOLD, YOU ARE TO THEM AS A VERY LOVELY SONG OF ONE WHO HAS A PLEASANT VOICE, AND CAN PLAY WELL ON AN INSTRUMENT; FOR THEY HEAR YOUR WORDS, BUT THEY DON'T DO THEM.
34 WHEN THIS COMES TO PASS, (BEHOLD, IT COMES), THEN SHALL THEY KNOW THAT A PROPHET HAS BEEN AMONG THEM.

You may feel, like Ezekiel, a very pleasant song but nothing much else. God endorses the prophetic by its results. One of the biggest ways to fast track is the word of knowledge because it is immediately measurable. A word of knowledge is a prophetic revelation of what is happening or has happened.

Most prophets avoid this area because a person can immediately tell you if you are right or not. However, Prophets by Office are particularly marked by an acute ability to speak words of knowledge. When you give accurate words of knowledge through risk, people immediately recognise your office.

JOHN 4:16-19
16 JESUS SAID TO HER, "GO, CALL YOUR HUSBAND, AND COME HERE."
17 THE WOMAN ANSWERED, "I HAVE NO HUSBAND." JESUS SAID TO HER, "YOU SAID WELL, 'I HAVE NO HUSBAND,'
18 FOR YOU HAVE HAD FIVE HUSBANDS; AND HE WHOM YOU NOW HAVE IS NOT YOUR HUSBAND. THIS YOU HAVE SAID TRULY."
19 THE WOMAN SAID TO HIM, "SIR, I PERCEIVE THAT YOU ARE A PROPHET.

6. REPEAT

Most prophets are afraid to do this final part, yet it is the most crucial part of the prophetic. Don't live off of the success of your last accurate word of knowledge or prophecy for a nation. Live a repetitious prophetic lifestyle without trapping yourself in performance. People afraid of this word 'repeat' are afraid because they have a performance mentality.

Performance mentality says:

- What if God doesn't speak to me as powerfully today as He did yesterday?
- What if I am wrong and I lose my track record for being accurate?
- Perhaps I should help God by looking for clues or

supplementing prophecies with social media.

When you are in performance mode, you make desperate decisions in an attempt to outdo your last big performance. Remember, prophecy is not a performance and God isn't going to always show off in every place you go to minister. Repetition doesn't mean that I try to outdo yesterday's results. Repetition means that I stay so true to what the Holy Spirit is revealing, it means that I am not going to frustrate myself with what He is not revealing. You are not in ministry to show off, you are in ministry to show God and prophecy always points to God.

To get out of performance, you must rid yourself of the mentality of right or wrong prophecy. "Oh no," you may have said, "I gave a wrong prophecy!"

This is not always the right conclusion. Most often the right conclusion is, accurate versus inaccurate interpretation. Most people jump to the assumption that they didn't hear God when the conclusion is most likely that they interpreted what God was saying inaccurately. When you shift your mind set like this then you shift the attention off of yourself and back on to God where it should be and as you lean on Him then He begins to direct your path.

PROVERBS 3:5-6
5 TRUST IN THE LORD WITH ALL YOUR HEART, AND DON'T LEAN ON YOUR OWN UNDERSTANDING.
6 IN ALL YOUR WAYS ACKNOWLEDGE HIM, AND HE WILL MAKE YOUR PATHS STRAIGHT.

As you repeat stewardship in honouring God by leaning on

Him, God will honour you in the sight of man.

1 SAMUEL 3:20
20 ALL ISRAEL FROM DAN EVEN TO BEERSHEBA KNEW THAT SAMUEL WAS ESTABLISHED TO BE A PROPHET OF THE LORD.

In closing, people don't remember you for what you did, they remember you for what you do!

GALATIANS 6:9
9 LET US NOT BE WEARY IN DOING GOOD, FOR WE WILL REAP IN DUE SEASON, IF WE DON'T FAINT.

ABOUT THE AUTHOR

Tomi Arayomi received the Lord Jesus at the age of 15 and began ministry at 16 years old serving as a pastor under Foundation Faith Church. He served there and planted 10+ churches on university campuses UK wide whilst studying Law at University of Hertfordshire. He was later recognised for his apostolic and prophetic anointing and commissioned under Christian International by Dr Bill Hammond and Dr Sharon Stone on the 13th November 2010 where he currently serves as one of its visionary leaders. Tomi Arayomi is an author of 6 compelling books and one of the Apostolic Overseers of My Church Windsor, which saw its inception in 2016 and is a thriving church community in the heart of Windsor United Kingdom. Tomi co directs a channel with Dr Sharon Stone called Prophetic Voice TV which was formed with a mission to train everyday people to hear the voice of God every day. It runs daily on Facebook at www.facebook.com/propheticvoicetv. Tomi is known for his prophetic anointing and his office for prophetic ministry has been recognised world wide by leaders within Government including the United Nations where he has frequently been invited.

Tomi Arayomi is a sought out Prophet to Nations and has prophesied the future of many Nations. He believes that God has called him to build Nations through the power of the prophetic word! He demonstrates this through his International itinerate ministry. Tomi believes in the restoration of Prophet and State. He often says that, 'the day will come where governments of Nations shall seek the prophets again!' Tomi has featured on Christian television and radio all over the world including:

Revelation TV
TBN
Praise World TV
Malawi Times
Channels Tv

He believes God has called him to the ministry of transformation on a personal level and on a National level. Together with his wife Tahmar and his son Harvey they believe they have been called to train people to be prophets and prophets to be people.

Tomi married his wife Tahmar on 18th April 2015. Tahmar is co-pastoring 'My Church Windsor' with him and Dr Sharon Stone. They have one son Harvey Jonah Arayomi and together they believe God has called them to restore the prophetic back to the Nations. Tomi Arayomi is the son of Dr Joseph and Dr Funke Arayomi, he has a twin brother Tobi Arayomi and sister Yetomiwa Arayomi.

Follow Tomi Arayomi on
Facebook : www.facebook.com/tomiarayomi
Twitter: www.twitter.com/tomiarayomi
Instagram: www.instagram.com/tomiarayomi
Website: www.tomiarayomi.org
Email: admin@tomiarayomi.org

MORE BY TOMI ARAYOMI

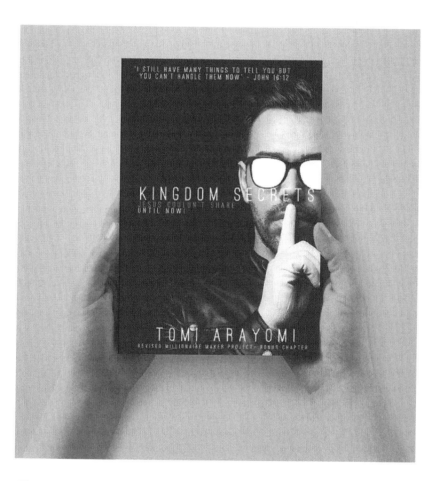

Purchase Tomi's books at www.tomiarayomi.org

COMING SOON...

COSMOPOLITAN
CHRISTIANITY

"WHAT IF THE ANSWER TO WOLVES DRESSED AS SHEEP
WILL BE SHEEP DRESSED AS WOLVES?"

TOMI ARAYOMI

26685007R00137

Printed in Great Britain
by Amazon